The Philosophy of Pāñcarātra

The Philosophy of Pāñcarātra

(An Advaitic Approach)

Dr. S. R. Bhatt

MOTILAL BANARSIDASS
INTERNATIONAL
DELHI

Reprint Edition: Delhi, 2023
Second Revised Edition: Delhi, 1980

ISBN : 978-81-19394-02-9

Also available at

MOTILAL BANARSIDASS INTERNATIONAL
H. O.- 41 U.A. Bungalow Road, (Back Lane)Jawahar Nagar, Delhi - 110 007
4261 (basement) Lane #3,Ansari Road, Darya Ganj, New Delhi - 110 002
203 Royapettah High Road, Mylapore, Chennai - 600 004
12/1A, 2nd Floor, Bankim Chatterjee Street, Kolkata - 700 073
Stockist : Motilal Books, Ashok Rajpath, Near Kali Mandir, Patna - 800 004

Printed in India
MOTILAL BANARSIDASS INTERNATIONAL

Dedicated

to

The Revered Memory of My Brother

Late Shri Kamaleshwar Bhatt

Foreword

The Pāñcarātra school has an important place exerting its great influence on the culture, philosophy and religion of India. It has a very ancient origin shrouded in mystery. The scholars have not given the same attention to the Āgama literature as they have done as regards the Vedic literature. Whatever notice has been taken of the Pāñcarātra literature by some eminent scholars both in the east and in the west, is not adequate. On this background the effort of Dr. S.R. Bhatt in presenting this comprehensive and critical study of the Pāñcarātra Philosophy deserves commendation. He has studied the original texts of the various important Saṁhitās like the Ahirbudhnya Saṁhitā, Viṣṇu Saṁhitā, Jayākhya Saṁhitā, Parameśwara Saṁhitā, Mārkaṇḍeya Saṁhitā, Padma Saṁhitā, Brahma Saṁhitā and also Viṣṇu Tantra, Lakṣmi Tantra and so on.

He has systematically dealt with the whole subject, starting with the historical introduction and the description of the Pāñcarātra literature and philosophy and gradually going to more details of the metaphysical problems of the nature of Ultimate Reality, the nature of the world, the nature and destiny of the individual self and the means of emancipation.

It is generally supposed that the Pāñcarātra teaching is more inclined towards Rāmānujācārya's Viśiṣṭādvaita than to Śaṅkarācārya's Advaita. It is the main contention of the present author in this study that it is a superficial understanding of the Pāñcarātra that has led to this misconception. He is of the firm opinion that in spite of some of the doctrines which are suggestive of the Viśiṣṭādvaita Philosophy, there is an overwhelming evidence in the texts which convincingly indicates the basic advaitic position of the Pāñcarātra school. This does not mean that the Pāñcarātra Philosophy is a bare copy of the Advaita system. There are deviations and modifications and additions which are not wholly in consonance with the Advaita Philosophy, and some of which come to be criticised severely from the Advaita standpoint, as for example, the doctrine of Vyūha. Nevertheless the Pāñcarātra teaching at its core and essence is unmistakably advaitic. The doctrine of the transcendent and Nirguṇa nature of the Ultimate Reality, the theories of bimbapratibimbavāda and avachchedavāda, the phenomenal nature of the world, the oneness and all-pervasiveness of the self, knowledge as the only efficient means of realization are some of the most fundamental teachings of the Pāñcarātra which abstracted from the theological-mythological accretions reveal the advaitic nucleus. The author has made some elaborate comparisons between the Pāñcarātra and the two schools of Vedānta and has convincingly shown how the teachings of Rāmānujācārya and Pāñcarātra fall apart and how those of the Advaita could be traced in the Pāñcarātra.

Those who are interested in this subject will certainly profit from a close study of this scholarly contribution.

A.G. JAVADEKAR

Contents

Opinions

Reviews in *The Hindu*

I

In this interesting book, Dr. S.R. Bhatt makes out a case for regarding the Pāñcarātra texts as advocating basically the truth of Advaita. The substance of his finding, in his own words is this: "The Pāñcarātra school believes in one ultimate non-dual Reality which possesses in its fundamental nature two aspects, viz. static (nivṛtti) and dynamic (pravṛtti) represented respectively by Brāhman and its Śakti. In the description of the former we find an unmistakable influence of the Advaitic tendency, and in the latter that of Sāṁkhya" (p. 9). That the world is an appearance is a basic tenet of Advaita. Dr. Bhatt cites support for this tenet in the Pāñcarātra literature. Even in the Nārada-Pāñcarātra, which is more inclined towards theism than the other texts, the world is characterised as illusory (mithyā). The power of māyā as in Advaita, is described as indeterminable, as neither real nor unreal. The realism of the Pāñcarātra thinkers is not real but only apparent. They are firm in emphasising the transcendental nature of the supreme being, and in showing that the changing world is incompatible therewith. In discussing the nature of the Jīva, the analogies of reflection in mirror and delimitation of ether are both given. The state of liberation of the individual soul is described in language which is thoroughly Advaitic employing typically Advaitic terms. Although there are non-Advaitic elements in the Pāñcarātra teaching, the predominance of the Advaitic tendency is unmistakable. Dr. S.R. Bhatt's conclusion on the evidence that he has been able to gather is "that the

Philosophy of the Pāñcarātra school is much nearer to Advaita than to Viśiṣṭādvaita" (p.10).

It is worthy of note that Dr. Bhatt himself recognises that he is not the first to have arrived at this conclusion. Sri P. T.S. Aiyangar seems to have held a similar view. The following words of his are quoted on p. 81 "The relation between the individual soul and the Paramātmā is much nearer the Advaitic position than would be palatable to the modern Viśiṣṭādvaitins."

Another point which should be borne in mind is that Dr. Bhatt is by no means sympathetic to Advaita. According to him, the Absolute of Advaita is static, inert and empty; the transcendence of the Absolute is emphasised at the cost of the reality of the world; there is no place for human values. And he gives it as his considered view that, in a true system of philosophy, instead of being annulled these values should be accepted as one of the available clues to the ultimate reality and that the true unity is not a static of a solitary self-centred Absolute but a dynamic unity of a society of souls realising their highest perfection in love and in mutually enriching fellowship.

It is not our present purpose to examine Dr. Bhatt's personal philosophical conviction. We have referred to this only with a view to show that he cannot be charged with a bias for Advaita and that his interpretation of the Pāñacarātra merits attention.

T.M.P. Mahadevan

II

The writer starts his preface to this book by saying, 'while working for my book "A study of Rāmānuja's System in comparison with Pāñcarātra school and Alwārs", I was struck by the remarkable similarity of the Pāñcarātra thought to the Advaitic Philosophy, a fact which seems to have been overlooked by the scholars.' The book provides ample evidence of the advaitic elements in the Pāñcarātra Āgama, for long thought to be purely Viśiṣṭādvaitic, in its underlying philosophy. After a historical introduction of the nature and origin of Pāñcarātra the author proceeds to consider the subjects of Ultimate Reality, the World, the Nature and Destiny of the Individual Self and the Means of Emancipation and proceeds to show that in all these there are unmistakable evidences in the Pāñcarātra text of Advaitic thought. The concepts of Nirguṇa Brahman, of the phenomenality of Īśvara, of Śakti, of the *Vibhutva* of the Jīva and of its identity with Brāhman and of *jñāna* as the sure means to *mokṣa* are found expounded at length in the texts.

There are remarkable similarities between Pāñcarātra and Advaita. Not only this, the author points out that there are elements of thought in the Pāñcarātra which are totally foreign to Rāmānuja's thought. The idea of the Jīva being an *aṁśa* of Brahman, the doctrine of multiplicity of Jīvas, the *vibhutva* of the Jīva in the state of freedom, the description of the state of release are all different from tenets of Rāmānuja's philosophy. The author further points out that the whole theory and practice of bhakti in Rāmānuja is essentially different from that of Pāñcarātra, so much so that psychologically speaking they may be said to be just the opposite.

We trust we have said enough about the contents of the book to whet the appetite of the reader in respect of a widely held view that the Pāñcarātra philosophy is mainly Viśiṣṭādvaitic. The author's thesis is that the opposite is the case, and he affirms this by quoting chapter and verse from the Āgamic Saṁhitās. This is a very revealing book which will repay careful study.

PROF. P. SANKARANARAYANNA

Preface

While working for my book 'A study of Rāmānuja's System in comparison with Pāñcarātra School and Ālwārs', I was struck by the remarkable similarity of the Pāñcarātra thought to the Advaita Philosophy, a fact which seems to have been overlooked by the scholars. Uptill now very little has been done by way of critical study of the Pāñcarātra philosophy except Dr. Schrader's book which is mostly confined to the historical and the cosmological aspects of the Saṁhitā thought. He has not dealt with the Nārāyaṇīya account of the Pāñcarātra thought, and his account of the Śamhitā thought also is not complete. Further, he has maintained non-advaitism as the teachings of the Saṁhitās, but my findings lead me to regard Advaitism as the view towards which the Saṁhitās incline.

Though the dominant trend of the Pāñcarātra thought is thus advaitic, its non-advaitic tendency need not be denied or explained away. But it must be noted that it is only a tendency and not the main motive. The only idea that has prompted me to bring out this work is to put forth the advaitic elements of the Pāñcarātra thought which have so far remained unnoticed. I hope this work will give some incentive to scholars to take up this problem for a more critical and exhaustive study.

I take this opportunity to express my sense of gratitude to Dr. A.G. Javadekar; but for his critical and constructive suggestion and guidance this work would not have been what it is. I must also express my thanks to Prof. T.P. Chitanand and Dr. S.L. Bhyrappa for going through the manuscript and offering their critical views.

Delhi : S.R. Bhatt
5-1-1980

CHAPTER I

HISTORICAL INTRODUCTION

1. Introduction

In the history of Vaishnavism the Pancharatra school-also known as Bhagavata, Sattvata, Ekantika etc.[1]—occupies a unique and very important place.It forms an important part of the Hindu Agama religion[2] which has exerted a strong influence all over the country, and has contributed a lot in making the 'living' Hindu religion thrive in the different parts of India under different names. Perhaps, it may come as a surprise to many that the popular faith and the actual opinions held and the religious practices performed by the devoted Hindus are taken entirely from the Agamas. Though the Agamas-especially their caryapada-may make an unpalatable reading, they are indispensable to the understanding of the whole of the later religious and philosophical literature of India.

The Hindu Agama religion[3] has branched off into three schools, viz., Vaishnava, Shaiva and Shakta, respectively with Vishnu, Shiva and Shakti as the 'presiding Deities' or 'sole Supreme'. The votaries of these sects believe that their Agamas are revealed by their respective Deities[4], and hence the word Agama. The Agama literature bears the stamp of pure theology, and teaches the ritual observances of these sects together with the underlying metaphysical and mystical principles.

Vedic literature has received a good deal of attention of the modern scholars, but Agama literature, which is equally important, has been given very little consideration. Apart from the scanty information given by F. Otto Schrader[5], no attempt has been made to undertake a critical study of the unexplored field of the Pancharatra which is now practically extinct. In a very few places in south India some considerable remnants of it are still being preserved and studied. A few samhitas only have been published by now, and quite a considerable portion of it remains unknown. The zealous guarding of this literature by the sectarians from the prying eyes of critical scholars and the apparent antipathy of the Vedic literature towards it on account of some of its revolting doctrines, are probably responsible for this.

2. Origin of the word 'Pancharatra'

It is very difficult to say why the name 'Pancharatra is given to this school. About the origin of this word' different interpretations and explanations are offered. One thing, however, is certain that this school has something to do with five 'ratras', but what these five 'ratras' are, is now merely a matter of conjecture. We give below some of the explanations usually proposed.

1. The word 'pancharatra' is a pretty old one and is mentioned for the first time in the Shatapatha Brahmana (XIII. 6. 1) where Purusha Narayana is said to have conceived the idea of Purusha-medha, which was otherwise called Pancharatra sattra (i.e. continued

sacrifice for five days) as a means of obtaining superiority over all beings and becoming all beings. Some scholars try to trace the origin of the name of this school to this particular event and maintain that the Pancharatra cult might have started as a part of the sacrificial cult of the Purusha Narayana. Though there is no evidence to this effect, it seems probable that the original adherents of this cult made sacrificial offerings five times a year (or a day) or observed some vows on five nights or seasons[6].

2. Another explanation put forth is that the name pancharatra is based on the five principal subjects treated in this system. It is so understood in the Narada Pancharatra[7] which says that five kinds of 'ratras' (disciplines) are discussed here, and hence the name. They are Tattva (Ontology), Muktiprada (Liberation), Bhaktiprada (Devotion), Yaugika (Yoga) and Vaishayika (Science). Though the five sections of the said Samhita accord rather imperfectly with this division, it is possible that the above view may rest on some good tradition.

3. There is a suggestion that the sect took its name from its central dogma which was the pancharatra sattra of Narayana interpreted philosophically as the five-fold manifestation of God by means of His Para, Vyuha, Vibhava, Antaryamin and Archa forms[8]. But it is possible to disprove this view on the basis of the Narayaniya (i.e. Mahabharata) account of the Pancharatra school, which enumerates only three manifestations.

Besides these explanations some quite fanciful explanations are also offered. For example :

1. The Narayaniya (339.107) says that the Pancharatra school is' so called because four Vedas and Samkhya-yoga are combined in it.

2. The Padma Tantra (I. I. 73) explains 'pancharatra' as meaning that which turns (i.e., obscures) the other five shastras into night. These five shastras being Shaiva, Samkhya, Yoga, Arhata and Bauddha[9].

3. The Shri-prashna Samhita (II. 40) interprets the word 'ratri' as nescience, and derives the word 'pancharatra' from the root 'pac' = to cook (destroy) meaning that which destroys ignorance.[10]

4. The Parama Samhita (I. 39-41) compares the five mahabhutas (physical senses of the embodied soul) to five nights. The shastra by the study of which all the five nights are destroyed is called pancharatra.[11]

5. The Ishvara Samhita (XXI. 52.582) says that the Pancharatra literature is so called because it embodies five lectures delivered by Narayana in five nights to five sages.[12]

6. The Shakti-sangama mentions that the followers of this school observe a vow in which the face of a Shiva devotee should not be seen for five successive nights and days.[13]

7. It is also suggested that this school got this name because it dwells upon five sacraments, viz., tapa, pundra, nama, mantra, and yaga.

8. It is also thought that this system advocates five modes of worship, viz., abhigamana, upadana, ijya, svadhyaya and yoga, and therefore it is so named.

From the above account it is clear that it is not easy to say why the term 'pancharatra' is used to denote this school. The very fact that several definitions are given, none agreeing with the other, shows that the later adherents of this school were themselves not sure of the meaning of this term, which became obscure in the course of time.

3. The origin and antiquity of the Pancharatra school

From the material available to us it is very difficult to find out precisely the antiquity of the Pancharatra as a school of thought and a body of people practising a mode of religion in conformity thereto. Though many conjectures have been put forth to trace its antiquity,[14] we can, at this stage, say only this much that it seems to be of considerable antiquity and its earliest literature must have been composed; perhaps in the North, long before the great epics.[15] Though we have no literary evidence as regards the line of reasoning by which the doctrines of this school came to be formulated and reached the present form, it is probable that there was a body of the pancharatra teaching, handed down from teacher to pupil, and practised, more or less, generally by the people before the general teachings got formulated in the handbooks.

4. The sources and extent of the Pancharatra literature

The earliest available record of the Pancharatra thought is contained in the Narayaniya section of the Shanti parvan of the Mahabharata. But there it does not seem to appear in its original form, because the sectaries have preserved for us not so much the opinion actually held by the people as the opinion the sectaries wished them to hold. Dr. Schrader has rightly opined that it does not give an impression of being based on first-hand knowledge[16].

Apart from the Narayaniya we find an exposition of the Pancharatra doctrines in a voluminous literature variously named as Pancharatra Upanishad,[17] Pancharatra Tantras,[18] Pancharatra Agamas, but popularly known as Pancharatra Samhitas[19] a major portion of which seems to be lost. The extensive nature of the Pancharatra literature can be gauged from what Dr. Schrader has said, "The Samhita literature of the Pancharatras must have once amounted to not less but probably more than one and a half million shlokas."[20] The Shri-Prashna (II.41) Vishnu-tilak (I. 140-145) and other texts mention that the original Pancharatra had one and a half crore of verses. Traditionaly 108 samhitas are mentioned. Dr. Schrader enumerates 215 and suggests that there may be many more.[21] The Lakshmi Tantra gives the number as 219.

5. The principal subjects treated in the Pancharatra literature

The teachings of the Pancharatra school, and in general of the whole Agama literature, generally fall into four sections, according to the four main themes treated which are as follows :—

(i) **Jnana**:—It comprises the philosophical doctrines regarding God, Nature, the individual soul, the process of creation, the means of liberation etc. It also includes occultism containing the knowledge of the secret powers of letters, syllables, formulas and figures.

(ii) **Yoga** :—It means meditation or concentration, specially with a view to acquire magic powers or to obtain release.

(iii) **Kriya** :—It includes the rules to be followed in the making of idols, and in the construction and consecration of temples.

(iv) **Charya** :—It deals with the rules of conduct regarding worship, rites, festivals and social duties.

Dr. Schrader[22] mentions ten principal subjects but suggests that the name pancharatra must have come from the five principal subjects treated in it, which are Tattva (Ontology), Muktiprada (Liberation), Bhaktiprada (Devotion), Yaugika (Yoga) and Vaishayika (Science). This suggestion we meet with in the Narada Pancharatra and Ahirbudhnya Samhita.[23]

The major part of the Pancharatra literature, however, comprises Kriya and Charya. Though all the principal topics mentioned above are not treated in every single work, all the samhitas somehow contain a medley of philosophy and occultism, mysticism and magic, rituals and ethics. As a matter of fact there is very little philosophy in them, because their main concern is to describe the rules of initiation, the holding of Vaishnava marks, ablution and purificatory rites, offerings and religious festivities, sacrificial oblations, expiation of sins, methods of remedy by incantations, funeral sacrifices, meditation, methods of self-control, description of images, rules regarding the making of images, installation of images, forms and ritualism of worship, and the uses, modes and efficacy of various mantras and rituals. Interspersed with these are philosophical doctrines which form the basis of the later Shri-vaishnava philosophy and religion.

6. The nature of the Pancharatra philosophy

The Pancharatra philosophy in the Narayaniya is comparatively less complicated than what it is in the Samhitas. It is free from the ritualistic and tantric details, Charya and the Kriya padas, which occupy more than three-fourths of the samhita literature. This is perhaps due to the early origin of the Narayaniya. Whatever ritualistic elements are found in the Narayaniya, are brahmanical in nature. The Narayaniya thought contains a curious combination of Upanishadic monism, proto-Samkhya dualism. proto-yoga mysticism, along with the popular worship of a personal God in an ardently devotional atmosphere, with all its paraphernalia of mythological fancy. The speculative side which is meant to supply a philosophical background to the religion, is a medley of various ideas, sometimes unrelated and incongruous.[24]

The primary concern of the Pancharatra school in the samhita literature seems to be the sadhana or the practical method of realising the ultimate Reality. Their aim is not to establish any definite system of thought. That is why abstract metaphysical speculations do not find prominence in them. The philosophical portions introduced here and there with a view to explain the various practices and rituals, are not very convincing and are not always relevant to them. The samhitas incorporate the fundamental tenets of other darshanas, mainly of the Vedanta and Samkhya-Yoga, and apply them to the practical effort for the realisation of the supreme goal.

The Pancharatra school believes in one ultimate non-dual Reality which possesses in its fundamental nature two aspects, viz., static (nivrtti) and dynamic (pravrtti) represented respectively by Brahman and its Shakti. In the description of the former we find an unmistakable influence of the Advaitic tendency, and in the latter that of Samkhya. The Ultimate Reality is described in the manner of the Upanishads as an attributeless conscious substance, always eluding and transcending intellectual comprehension and verbal expression. This attitude of silence and ineffability is perfectly in line with its predominating advaitic tendency. We cannot, therefore, but believe (though it would be quite unpalatable to a vishishtadvaitin) that the philosophy of the Pancharatra school is much nearer to Advaita than to Vishishtadvaita.[25]

7. Tantric element in the Pancharatra

The most dominant element and a notable feature of the Pancharatra samhitas seems to be the prevalence of tantrism. It is not yet definitely known how and when tantrism arose, but that it is of considerable antiquity, no one can deny. It seems purely of non-Vedic origin. Its ideas and practices are frankly anti-Vedic. In its early character it does not seem to have recognised the authority of the Vedas, though in later times it could not ignore them.

The extant samhitas are, perhaps, the earliest available records of the tantric influence. How deeply tantric ideas and practices have influenced the Pancharatra could be seen from an examination of the contents of the samhitas like Jayakhya, Parameshvara, Ahirbudhnya etc. which are the most ancient and authoritative Pancharatra works.[26]

The Ahirbudhnya Samhita is full of lore on the tantric mantras.[27] Chapters 51 to 59 of this Samhita are full with the explanations of the vaishnava mantras and the linguistic occultism from subtle and highest stand-points. It clearly declares that the Pancharatra is based partly on the Vedic[27] and partly on the tantric system.[28] It believes in the esoteric nature of the mantras and regards the world as created through them. The world has come into being from the Sudarshana power and all the natural, physical and other kinds of energies and powers of all things in the world are but its manifestations.[29] It describes the mantras as the energy of Vishnu which is pure consciousness. This energy is called variously as Kriya-shakti, Samarthya, Yoga, Parameshthya, Mahatejasa, Maya etc.[30] The Jayakhya samhita gives a different account of the process of creation through the mantras. Here the creative tattvas are said to proceed from their respective consonants of the alphabet.[31]

8. The Pancharatra school and Vedic authority

Before we conclude the historical survey of the Pancharatra school it will not be out of place to discuss here the time-honoured controversy regarding the relation between the Vedic and the Pancharatra teachings. There has been considerable discussion as to whether the Pancharatra is Vedic or non-Vedic in origin and pro-Vedic or anti-Vedic in attitude. Among the writers of Smrtis, Puranas and Dharmashastras it is curious to find that while some of them are fanatically in favour of the Pancharatra, others are quite outspoken and vehement in their condemnation of it. The votaries of the latter section which perhaps consisted of orthodox brahmins consistently maintained that there are fundamental differences between the Vedas and the Pancharatra, and that the Pancharatra is non-Vedic in origin and anti-Vedic in attitude, and hence deserving of condemnation. Against this section we find a long array of Sri-Vaishnava and later Pancharatra writers who make a strenuous effort to disprove the charge of unorthodoxy on the Pancharatra. (For details see my paper in Hindi स्मृतिकाल में वैदिक और पाञ्चरात्र विचारधारा का संबंध-काशी नागरी प्रचारिणी पत्रिका-संवत् 2021 अंक-3)

From the ambiguous pronouncements on this problem by the authors of the Pancharatra works it cannot be ascertained whether they based their teachings on the Vedas or gave their own views and passed them on as being based on the Vedas. Most of them regard the Pancharatra as in conformity with the Vedas, but, curiously enough, sometimes they regard the Vedas as the roots,[32] and sometimes as the shoots[33] of the Pancharatra. From the contents of the Samhita literature I find it difficult to agree with Dr. S. N. Dasgupta's view that the Pancharatra doctrines are associated with the Purusha-sukta of the Rigveda and the Shatapatha Brahmana (Xiii. 6. 1.) mainly because except the philosophical portion which is borrowed from the Upanishads and the Samkhya-Yoga, the major part of the Pancharatra literature is manifestly non-Vedic. The anti-Vedic attitude of the Pancharatra is also manifest at some places[34] where Vedas are regarded as inferior to the Pancharatra. But being in a minority the Pancharatra followers dared not revile the Veda and had to be conciliatory. They took great pains to reconcile the differences. In order to give a Vedic basis for the non-Vedic Pancharatra they traced the origin of their school to an unknown Vedic school called Ekayana-a sect of the Kanva shakha of the Shukla Yajurveda

(The word Ekayana is derived from the Vedic passage, *Nanyao pantha ayanaya vidyate*). This Ėkayana was further identified with the Ekayana shastra mentioned in the Chandogya upanishad. (vii. 1. 2.)[35] A similar attempt was made to derive the etymology of the word pancharatra from the Pancharatra sattra of the Shatapatha Brahmana (XIII. 6. 1).

This conciliatory attitude of the pancharatra followers resulted in the softening of its outright condemnation in the brahmin circles and consequently the Pancharatra was regarded as authoritative in so far as it did not come into conflict with the Vedas.[36] It should be noted that the extreme orthodox section of the brahmins, however, did not accept this reconciliation.[37]

From the foregoing it appears that the prescription of the early Pancharatra were not at all favourable to the brahminic tradition, and that because of their non-Vedic origin and anti-Vedic attitude they were vehemently condemned and deprecated. But latter on when the school altered its attitude and amended its doctrines and practices, it was given a place under Vedic orthodoxy but that was an inferior one only.

References and foot-notes :

1. In the Padma-tantra—a sacred canon of the Pancharatra school—the following synonyms of the Pancharatra are given :

सुरिसुहृद् भागवतास्सात्त्वताः पञ्चकालवित् ।
ऐकान्तिकाः तन्मयाश्च पञ्चरात्रिका इत्यपि ॥ IV. 2-88.

'cf.' Mahabharata XII. 335-19 ; 348-4. etc.

2. The word 'आगम' is derived from the root 'गम्' with prefix 'आ' (आङ्+गम्+अच्) meaning 'that which has come' or 'revealed.'

आगतं पञ्चवक्त्रात्तु गतं च गिरिजानने ।
सुमतं वासुदेवस्य तस्मादागममुच्यते ॥

or शिववक्त्रादम्बुजायातं पारम्पर्यं क्रमेण तु ।
छंदोलक्षण संसिद्धमागममित्यभिधीयते ॥ (पिंगलमतम्)

However, two different explanations of the word 'आगमं' are also found, viz.,

(i) आज्ञावत्तु समन्ताच्च गम्यते इति आगमो मतः ।

(ii) आगच्छन्ति बुद्धिमारोहन्ति यस्यादभ्युदय निःश्रेयसोपायः स आगमः । तत्त्ववैशारदी of वाचस्पति मिश्र ।

The Shabdakalpadruma enumerates the following characteristics of Agama literature :—

सृष्टिश्च प्रलयश्चैव देवतानां तथार्चनम् ।
साधनं चैव सर्वेषां पुरश्चरणमेव च ॥
षट्कर्म साधनं चैव ध्यानयोगश्चतुर्विधः ।
सप्तभिर्लक्षणैर्युक्तं त्वागमं तद्विदुर्बुधाः ॥

The Agamas are styled by their followers as 'shruti' and are regarded as equally or even more authoritative than the Vedas. See infra f. n. 34.

3. Bauddha and Jaina religions also have their own Agamas.

4. See supra f. n. 2.

5. See Introduction to the Pancharatra and the Ahirbudhnya Samhita, Adyar, 1916.

6. पञ्चरात्रि व्रतं प्राप्ता पञ्चरात्रा प्रकीर्तिताः ।

7. रात्रं च ज्ञानवचनं ज्ञानं पञ्चविधं स्मृतम् ।

I. 1. 44, cf. अहिर्बुध्न्य I. 64

8. तत्परव्यूह विभव स्वभावादि निरुपणम् ।
पाञ्चरात्राह्वयं तन्त्रं मोक्षक फललक्षणम् ।।

अहि. XI. 64

9. (अ) पञ्चेतराणि शास्त्राणि रात्रीयन्ते महान्त्यपि ।

(आ) पञ्चत्वमथवा यद्वत् दीव्यमाने दिवाकरे ।
ऋच्छन्ति रात्रयः तद्वत् इतराणि तदन्तिके ।।

10. रात्रिरज्ञानमित्युक्तं पञ्चेत्यज्ञाननाशनम् ।

11. (अ) महाभूतगुणाः पञ्चरात्रयो देहिनः स्मृताः ।
तद्योगाद्विनिवृत्तिर्वा पञ्चरात्रमिति स्मृतम् ।।
भूतमात्राणि गर्वश्च बुद्धिरव्यक्तमेव च ।
रात्रयः पुरुषस्योक्ता पञ्चरात्रं ततस्स्मृतम् ।।

(आ) रात्रयो गोचरा पंच शब्दादि विषयात्मिकाः ।
महाभूतात्मका वाऽत्र पञ्चरात्रमिदं ततः ।।
अवाप्य तु परमतेजो यत्रैताः पञ्चरात्रयः ।
नश्यन्ति पञ्चरात्रं तत् सर्वाज्ञान विनाशनम् ।। (विष्णुसंहिता)

(इ) वियद्वायुश्च वह्निश्च आपश्चैव धरास्तथा ।
रात्रयो देहिनः प्रोक्ता अविद्या संभवास्मृताः ।।
तद्योगाद्विनिवृत्तं तु कारयेदुर्वस्तुतः ।
पाञ्चरात्रमिदं प्रोक्तं एतच्छास्त्रंमया तदा ।। (विष्णुतन्त्र)

12. आद्यमेकायनं वेदं रहस्याम्नाय संज्ञितम् ।
दिव्यमन्त्रक्रियोपेत मोक्षकफल लक्षणम् ॥
पञ्चायुधांस्ते पञ्च शांडिल्यौपगायनः ।
मौञ्जायनः कौशिकश्च भारद्वाजश्च योगिनः ॥

पञ्चापि प्रथगेकं दिवारात्रं जगत्प्रभुः ।
अध्यापयामास यतः तदेतन्मुनिपुंगवान् ॥
शास्त्रं सर्वजनैर्लोके पञ्चरात्रमितीर्यते ।

13. पञ्चरात्रि व्रतं प्राप्ता पञ्चरात्रा प्रकीर्तिताः ।
दिनपञ्चकपर्यन्तं शैवानां न विलोकनम् ॥
वर्तन्ते वैष्णवा ये च शिवनिंदा परायणाः ।

14. See Foreword to the Jayakhya Samhita—Gaekwar's Oriental Series pp. 13-16; see also—prastavana of the same Pp. 42-47.

15. See. Schrader. Loc. cit. P. 16.

16. Ibid P. 15.

17. Ibid P. 18.

18. Regarding the derivation of the word 'tantra' opinions differ. One suggestion is that the word tantra comes from 'tantu' (thread) and is a translation of the Tamil word 'nul' meaning work. On this hypothesis it is suggested that the Agamas are the Sanskrit translations of the original Tamil works which are lost. They seem to understand Agamas not as revelations but as works which have come from other languages, viz., Tamil. But this hypothesis has found favour with only a few.

In Kashika-vritti, tantra is derived from the root 'tan', to spread, with the suffix 'tran'

तनुते त्रायते नित्यं तन्त्रमित्थं विदुर्बुधाः ।

The Vishnu Samhita utilising the same etymology explains it differently as,

सर्वेऽर्था येन तन्यन्ते त्रायन्ते च भयाज्जनाः ।

इति तन्त्रस्य तन्त्रत्वं तंत्रज्ञाः परिचक्षते ॥

or तनोति विपुलार्थानि तत्त्वमन्त्र समन्वितान् ।

त्राणं च कुरुते यस्मात् तंत्रमित्यभिधीयते ॥

The word tantra had a very wide meaning and was used loosely to denote any kind of scientific or philosophical treatise which was more modern than the Vedic literature, e.g., Nyaya-tantra, Yoga-tantra, Dharma-tantra etc. Later on it was generally used in an exclusive sense to denote a body of writings comprehending the whole culture of a certain epoch in diverse directions such as, religion, rites, rituals, ceremonies, law, medicine and so forth.

The following characteristics of tantra are enumerated in the Varaha tantra :—

सर्गश्च प्रतिसर्गश्च मन्त्र निर्णय एव च ।

हरचक्रस्याख्यानं स्त्रीपुंसोश्चैव लक्षणम् ॥

राजधर्मो दानधर्मो युगधर्मस्तथैव च ।

व्यवहार कथ्यते च तथा चाध्यात्मवर्णनम् ।

इत्यादि लक्षणैर्युक्तं तन्त्रमित्यभिधीयते ॥

19. The word samhita is derived from the root-'dha' with 'sam' to put together, to unite, which means a metrical composition or a collection of sacred texts

2

dealing with various topics of religion, ritual, law, medicine and so forth. In the Paushkara Samhita (40.156) it is said that any work extending to the figure of 12000 verses can be called a Samhita.

20. Loc. cit. p. 14.

21. Ibid Pp. 6-12.

22. Ibid P. 26

23. रात्रं च ज्ञान वचनं ज्ञानं पञ्चविधं स्मृतम् । अहि. I. 54

24. See Indian Historical Quarterly 1931, Pp. 346-58. 1932, Pp. 64-84.

25. Jayakhya Samhita IV. 83-6 ; V. 29, Parama Samhita II. 87-90.

26. Interested readers may see the introductions to the published volumes of the Jayakhya and the Parameshvara Samhitas.

27. पञ्चरात्रमयी दिव्या सांख्ययोगादिसम्मिता ।
संहितेयं महामुह्या नानामन्त्रमयीपरा ॥ 59. 70

28. वेदतन्त्रमयोद्भूता नाना प्रसवशालिनी । VI. 9

29. Ibid XVI. 4-6.

30. साक्षाद्विष्णोः क्रियाशक्तिः शुद्धा संविन्मयी परा । XVI. 10

31. Chapter VI. 9 to 17, 220-228.

32. श्रुतिमूलमिदं शास्त्रं प्रमाणं कल्पसूत्रवत् । मार्कण्डेय संहिता P. 6
cf. विष्णुतन्त्र I. 36, पारमेश्वर-ज्ञानपाद I. 18.
मूल वेदानुसारेण प्रोक्तानि हितकाम्यया ।
ईश्वर संहिता I. 50 cf. विष्णु संहिता II. 11.

33. महतो वेदवृक्षस्य मूलभूतो महानयम् ।
स्कन्दभूता ऋगाद्यास्ते शाखा भूतास्तथामुने ।
ईश्वर संहिता I. 24 cf. पारमेश्वरसंहिता I. 76.

34. वेदमेकायनं नाम वेदानां शिरसि स्थितम् । श्रीप्रश्नसंहिता II. 38
उत्तमा पञ्चरात्रस्था मध्यमास्तु त्रयी मयाः । लक्ष्मीतंत्रXXII. 36

35. एषः एकायनो वेदः प्रख्यातः सात्वतो विधिः ।
मोक्षायनाय वैपन्था एतदन्यो न विद्यते ॥
पारमेश्वर I, 56. cf. ईश्वर संहिता I. 19 ; XXI, 531.
काण्वीं शाखामधीयानां वेदवेदान्त पारगान् ।
ईश्वर संहिता XXI. 554, cf. जयाख्य I. 109.
See. काण्व शाखा महिमा संग्रह of नागेश-Madras Government Oriental Library-Triennial Catalogue III. I. B. P. 3299.

36. तत्र वेदाविरुद्धांशों अप्युक्तः क्वचित् क्वचित् ।
वैदिकैस्तत् ग्रहणे दोषो न भवत्येव कर्हिचित् ॥
देवीभागवत VII. 39. 31.
पाञ्चरात्र पाशुपतादिन्यपि शास्त्राणि वेदाविरुद्धं
प्रमाणमेवेति पारिजातः । कत्यरत्नाकर P. 37
तथा च योंशो मार्गाणां वेदेन न विरुध्यते सोंशः
प्रमाणमित्युक्तं केषांचिद् । सत संहिता IV. 4, 16

37. धर्मं शुद्धिमभिप्सद्भिर्न वेदादन्यदिष्यति ।
धर्मस्य कारणं शुद्धं मिश्रमन्यत्प्रकीर्तितम् ॥
अतः स परमो धर्मः यः वेदादवगम्यते ।
अवरः स तु विज्ञेयः यः पुराणादिषु स्थितः ॥
Vyasa quoted by Apararka in Comm. on Yajnavalkya Smriti p. 3; cf. Devi Bhagavata XI. I. 21-23.
पुराणेषु स्मृतिविरुद्धाचाराणां बहुषो दर्शनात्
व्यवहारमयूख P. 98

CHAPTER II

THE NATURE OF THE ULTIMATE REALITY

Introduction

The demand for some kind of pronouncement on the nature of Reality is one which the human mind cannot help making. But there seems to be nothing more hazardous for the human speculation than to offer a universally acceptable conception of it. The conclusions of logic leave us with the idea of one Being, an all-inclusive Absolute, other than which there is none. But the facts of experience, on the other hand, compel us to admit a plurality of existence which cannot be cribbed and confined into the narrow limits of a rigid unity. Our dilemma is that we connot help believing in the existence of one fundamental all-inclusive Unity, while at the same time we cannot afford to deny the existence of the manifest Plurality. The problem, therefore, is, in what relation does the Plurality stand to the all-inclusive Unity ? Is the Unity the sole Reality and the Plurality merely nugatory ? To state the problem in concrete terms, what is the status of the world of animate beings and inanimate things in the scheme of Reality ? As a corollary to the problem of the nature of the Ultimate Reality is the issue whether the Absolute of philosophy is the same as the God of religion. In other words, does the Ultimate Reality denote a personal being who thinks and loves ? All these questions have been considered by the Pancharatra thinkers and we shall attempt a study of them here.

The two-fold aspects of the Supreme Being

The highest Reality, in the Pancharatra school is referred to as Parabrahman, a term which is the same as the Nirguna Brahman of the Upanishads. Like Shankara, the Pancharatra school makes a distinction between the Absolute of philosophy and the God of religion, the unconditioned Brahman and Brahman as conditioned by Maya, the intuitional Highest and the logical Highest, the metaphysically Real and the meditationally Ideal. Though such a distinction is drawn between the transcendent and the immanent aspects of the Supreme Being, and though both the impersonal and the personal forms are recognised, the Pancharatra school, unlike Shankara, is not at all clear about the ontological status of the personal or immanent aspect. The only Supreme Being the Pancharatra thinkers know of is the transcendent One. But, somehow, they cannot rest content with this aspect and soon recognise that aspect also with which the Supreme Being stands related to the universe. Of these two aspects, the transcendent one is undoubtedly real, but it is not clear as to whether both of them are equally real or the former alone is real. Nor is it clear whether the personal God has a being for Himself and an appearance for others. In the Narayaniya account we come across a passage[1] wherein it is stated that this later personal appearance is due to Maya, and should not be regarded as real. In the Samhitas we do not find any such clear statement, yet on the basis of the overall teaching of the school, which is Advaitic, we may aver that the personal form is regarded as real from meditational standpoint only.

Knowledge of the Supreme Being

Like Shankara, the Pancharatra school regards the ultimate Reality as unknown and unknowable through empirical reason. In the Narayaniya, Brahman is regarded as having a transcendent nature which is beyond the reach of human understanding. 'It is without end, without beginning and without middle; whose middle is unmanifest, who is beyond the Ken of logic or argument; who is unknowable.'[2] At times imitating the Upanishadic style Brahman is described as one 'that cannot be seen with the eye, touched with the sense of touch, smelt with the sense of smell, and It is beyond the ken of the sense of taste.'[3] The Jayakhya Samhita shares the same view but adds that though It is 'beyond the ken of eyes' It can be intuited directly like the fragrance of a flower.[4]

Though the transcendent aspect is thus unknowable and unmanifest, the immanent aspect is not so. The Narayaniya declares that the Deity reveals Himself to His devotees.[5] For instance the avyakta (impersonal) Brahman becomes vyakta (personal) Deity for the sake of Narada.[6] The Deity 'incapable of being seen by any one else showed Himself to His worshipper, the King Uparichara.'[7] But He was not manifest to the priest Brihaspati, who was indignant at seeing Him. He was told that only he can see God to whom He becomes gracious.[8]

Ekata, Dvita and Trita practised austerities for four thousand years, but could not see Him, and were told that He could not be seen by onè who lacked devotion.[9] He can be seen only by those who are Ekantins, i.e., devoted to Him wholly and solely.[10]

In this way the Pancharatra school believes that the unknown and incomprehensible becomes known and comprehensible, appears in human form, speaks through human tongue, solely out of the urge to save the devotee through grace. This is the wonder of wonders, the great mystery hidden even from great thinkers, but revealed to devotees like Narada and Uparichara. It should, however, be noted that Shankara also deals with the love of and devotion to the Deity (Ishvara).[11]

Nature of the Supreme Being in the Narayaniya

In the description of the nature of the Supreme Being in the Narayaniya we find a mingling of incongruous ideas. Narayana is sometimes identified with the Upanishadic Neuter Brahman and sometimes identified with the Supreme Purusha on the theistic pattern.[12] This is Perhaps because of the confusion of the two-fold aspects of Brahman mentioned above. That is why in speaking of the Supreme Being also the Narayaniya uses terms such as Vasudeva, Kshetrajna, Ishvara, Narayana, Mahapurusha etc.

The Narayaniya describes Brahman as unborn, eternal, everlasting, attributeless and impartite.[13] It is subtle, unknowable, unmanifest, unmoving, firm and beyond the senses.[14] It is all-pervading witness and the Inner Self of the whole world, yet It cannot be comprehended by any one at any time.[15] The all-Pervading nature of Brahman is described in such a way as to imply the idea that It is the only real and all are but reflections of It.[16] Though It is bodiless, It is said to pervade all the bodies.[17] Though originally unmanifest, It is said also to become manifest. This manifestation, as we have seen, is due to Maya, a term which recalls the expression 'atmamayaya' of the Gita. All this description is thoroughly Upanishadic, and is in consonance with the Advaitic tendency of the school. In the language of the Upanishads Brahman is described as with attributes as well as without attributes.[18] But more often It is referred to as 'nirguna' and 'nirgunatmakah'. It is described as being above the three prakrita gunas.[19]

Brahman is regarded as unmoving and hence actionless.[20] So It cannot be the direct creator of the world. When God is described as the creator,[21] we should understand that the reference is to the personal God and not to the Impersonal Absolute.

In the chapter 339, the Narayaniya enumerates about two hundred predicates of the Deity, and He is identified with the Absolute and with everything that symbolises greatness and perfection. This may be an indication that there is no ontological but only a conceptual difference between the Deity and the Absolute. Shankara also has maintained the same view.

Attributes of the Supreme Being

In the non-dualistic fashion the Supreme Being is very often described as 'jnanam', 'only mind', 'Lord of speech', 'The embodiment of correctness of judgement', 'identifiable with the wisdom of the Samkhya-yoga' and 'the preceptor of the Universe'[28] etc. It is further stated that when all things have perished knowledge remains as the sole companion of the Supreme Being.[23]

The above, perhaps, is the description of the unconditioned Brahman. The perfection of Brahman as conditioned is said to consist in love.[24] The loving nature of the Deity, which results in His friendly helpfulness, infinite tenderness and grace to the sinner-a characteristic of Vishnu even in the Rigvedic times-also features prominently in the Narayaniya. It is stated that through the grace of the Deity king Vasu ascended to heaven, a spot that is even higher than the region of Brahma Himself[25], and by His grace the King was rescued when thrown down from the heaven by a curse of the Rishis.[26] He is regarded as 'the granter of every wish' and His troops go everywhere for protecting His worshippers[27]. He is 'gracious' to all His worshippers', 'fond of them', ever-affectionate towards them.[28] He is the greatest friend[29] and the sole refuge to all men[30]. He dispels the fears of all persons.[31] From Him springs the attribute of forgiveness.[32]

Besides Knowledge and love the Deity is said to be righteousness-incarnate. He is regarded as perfect in the highest ethical sense since He has completed all vows and ceremonies mentioned in the Vedas.[33] He is the embodiment of one who has not fallen away from the yoga.[34] He is beyond all pairs of attributes and free from all attachments.[35] He is unpolluted by good or bad actions.[36] He establishes law and in order to set the standard for men, conforms to them Himself.[37] The Deity is made to declare, I have never uttered anything base or anything that is obscene. The Divine Sarasvati who is truth's self, and is otherwise known as Rta, represents my speech, and always dwells in my tongue.[38] I have never swerved from the attribute of Sattva (goodness).[39] I always hear words that are pure and holy and never catch anything that is sinful. Hence I am called 'Shuchishravas'.[40] Even the very names of the Deity have a sanctifying and cleansing Power.[41] The verse with which this discourse ends, is noteworthy in this connection. "There is nothing holier on earth, or in heaven, and nothing higher than Narayana. Having listened to this discourse, we feel that we have been cleansed from all our sins, and sanctified completely."[42]

Forms of the Deity

The Supreme Brahman is formless, but the Deity, Its conditioned and personal aspect, is said to possess a bewitchingly beautiful form, full of effulgence and glory. He is described as the illustrious

Deity with a thousand rays.[43] The beauty of the Deity is said to be indescribable and its nature is indicated only by means of inadequate analogies. Since this description does not interest us because of our philosophical treatment, I refrain from giving an account of it. Interested readers may refer to Chapter 340.

Abode of the Deity

The Narayaniya does not contain a clear account of the abode of the Supreme Being. At one place Badrikashrama is described as the abode of the Lord Narayana, but there the Lord is Himself said to be worshipping 'mulam prakrtim' (Original prakruti) which is said to reside in the Shvetadvipa situated in the Kshirasagara. Sometimes the Lord Narayana is described as residing in the Centre of Surya in whose rays reside innumerable munis (sages) and deities 'like birds perching on the branches of trees'[43] The whole account is infused with mythological fancy and religious mystery. It seems that the Lord Narayana stands for the personal God only.

Manifestations of the Deity

Unlike the later Samhitas which refer to the five-fold manifestations, the Narayaniya mentions three-fold manifestations of the Deity. The supreme Being is absolutely transcendent, to whom perhaps the phrase 'Mula prakrti' is applied. Its first immanent manifestation is Vasudeva or Narayana, the highest personal God. The second manifestation consists of three vyuhas. The third and the last manifestation are the vibhavas or avataras.

Vyuha manifestations

The doctrine of vyuha which we find fully elaborated in the Samhitas, is found in germ here. Here it is described not in a consistent manner. Varied accounts are given in chapters 339. 72-74; 340. 28ff; 341. 13-17; 344. 14ff; 347. 17ff; 348. 57-58; 351. 12ff etc.

This doctrine forms a part of the cosmic process of creation. The universe is supposed to evolve in two parallel and graduated orders, viz. a physical order of material causation, on the Samkhya pattern, and a spiritual order of conditioned existences, which is named as vyuha.[44] In this spiritual order of conditioned existences, the Supreme Being exists first as Vasudeva, and then in combination with the primeval matter (Avyakta cf. Mahat of Samkhya) appears as Jiva, called Samkarshana. By Samkarshana's spontaneous act there evolves from him Pradyumna, as mind of all creatures. (cf. Buddhi of Samkhya). From Pradyumna arises Aniruddha, as consciousness of all creatures (cf. Ahamkara of Samkhya). The Deity, then, becomes four-fold (chaturmurtidhara).[45] This account of vyuha doctrine has come under severe attack from Shankara in the Shariraka Bhashya under "Uttpattyasambhavadhikarana."[46]

Avatara Manifestations

The Narayaniya further mentions the theory of avataras which is more or less Pauranic only, with this difference that whereas in the Puranas the Supreme Being Itself takes incarnation and descends, here the incarnations do not proceed from the Supreme Being directly but only through the vyuhas. The motive behind the incarnation is said to be the good of creatures, restoration of righteousness and destruction of Asuras and evil elements. It mentions Varaha, Nrsimha, Aditya, Vamana, Kashvapa, Rama, Krishna, Hamsa, Kurma, Matsya and Kalkin,[47] as the various avataras of God.

Nature of the Supreme Being—In the Samhitas

The pure monism of the early Upanishadic thinkers was developed into a Monotheism in later Upanishads, and the Supreme Being first regarded as Nirguna etc., came to be thought of in religious terms as Saguna. The same process by which religion steps in to clothe the Absolute of philosophy with devotion and its paraphernalia, is observable to a much greater extent in the Samhitas. The description of the nature of the Supreme Being in Its transcendent aspect and the qualities predicated of It here are essentially the same as those given in the Upanishads, a fact which suggests that here an intensively ardent religion seeks to find support in the speculations of the Upanishadic sages.

The Ultimate Reality in the transcendent aspect is named as Param Brahma (or Para Brahman), a term which recalls the Upanishadic Nirguna Brahman. Brahman is described as originally unmanifest and impersonal, but subsequently assuming personal form.[48] In Its original nature It is beginningless and endless, eternal and immutable, and cannot be characterised either as existent or non-existent.[49] It is timeless,[50] nameless,[51] beyond past, present and future. It is neither before nor behind, neither below nor above, neither short nor long, neither gross nor atomic.[52] It is beyond all dvandvas (dualities), unique, unparallelled, supreme, highest. No similes apply to It and it can only be referred to as 'is'[53]. It is all-tranquil, unchanging, unpolluted, eternal, unmoving, non-active and unruffled like a waveless sea.[54] It is self-existent and the support of all other things.[55]

Its essence is pure consciousness and pure bliss. It is devoid of all that is evil and the abode of all that is good and blissful. It is beyond all prakrta gunas and yet is hidden by gunas (gunaguhya).[56]

It is the Supreme Existence and pervades all things, resides everywhere and in all things.[57]

All this description of the nature of the Ultimate Reality is purely Upanishadic, Advaitic and Monistic in character. There can be no doubt about the thoroughgoing Advaitic character of these utterances of the Samhitas. The unmistakable influence of Advaita on the Samhitas can further be made clear by a detailed analysis of each of the important Samhitas.

The Padma Samhita describes Brahman as follows, "Brahman is characterised by bliss; It is beginningless, changeless, always undifferentiated, self-knowing, faultless, superlatively subtle, self-determined, the ruler, self-luminous, spotless, infinite, indestructible, tranquil, invisible, capable of evolving the world, unchangeable, full of consciousness of bliss (cidananda), the essence of consciousness (cidrupa), omnipresent, supreme; devoid of past and future, the Lord called Vasudeva, the source of all beings, Ishvara, the Supreme Purusha of a stainless nature, eternal, without waves, without disturbance, boundless, beyond the gunas, with gunas, the giver of all desires."[58] The last line and a few subsequent lines are very much similar to the description of Brahman in the Gita XIII. It is noteworthy that the word saccidananda so frequently used in the Advaita as the description of Brahman, occurs here[59].

The Advaitic nature of the Pancharatra philosophy is further confirmed by the Lakshmi Tantra which describes Brahman as follows. "It is characterised by the absence of pain...It is the eternal by whom all this moving and motionless world is embraced... All this world is enveloped by Its ahamta (egoity). It is everywhere, tranquil, changeless, eternal, infinite, devoid of limitations of space, time etc. It is called Mahavibhuti, because It is Brahma, the supreme abode, the light without substratum, of six qualities, similar to the ocean, of immortality, waveless, shining. It is one undifferentiated consciousness, tranquil, free from rising and setting. It is called Brahma, the secondless, being possessed of Shakti, which is not different from It."[60]

The Jayakhya Samhita equally reveals its Advaitic tendency. It describes Brahman as supreme existence which is all-pervasive. All things are but reflections of It and It is the essence of all.[61] Just as fire resides in a lump of iron as separate and yet as inseparable, in the same way the highest Brahman resides in everything as a separate entity, and yet in an inseparable condition. Just as in a clean mirror whatever things are seen do not belong to the mirror, similarly the material world which is reflected in Brahman does not belong to It. In this world of deception Brahman pervades everything and yet is not attached to anything just as a drop of water on the leaf of a lotus."[62] "Its movement and fixity are like the empty space of a pot, which when carried appears to carry the space along with it, but in reality the space does not move anywhere with the movement of the pot. Similar is the case with Brahman. Wherever there is space there is air, and hence the two are identical, in the same way Brahman is identical with all the bhutas (elements)".[63]

The drishtantas of mirror and space are the stock examples of the Advaita school and are borrowed here. This is a clear instance of the Advaitic nature of the Pancharatra philosophy. The world is recognised here as a reflection, which is unreal, or as a conditioned aspect of Brahman. Here we find elements of both the Advaitic theories of Bimbaprati-bimbavada and Avacchedavada.

The Parama Samhita is also equally clear on the Advaitic character of the Pancharatra philosophy. It says, 'The self-same glorious bright One, the Supreme, the Highest Soul, manifests Itself in different forms, in various classes of beings. The manner in which a crystal bead, by the proximity of things of different colours, is seen in different colours, in the same way the Supreme Purusha, though one Itself, assumes in this world different forms according to the ingredient qualities, and thus becomes the bound ones and the released."[64] This passage is notable for its declaration that the one and the only Reality appears manifold. This appearance is compared to the unreal varied appearance of the crystal bead. Lastly it declares that the finite soul, bound or released, is none else but Brahman.

The Ahirbudhnya Samhita also describes the Ultimate Reality in the Advaitic manner. The Ultimate Reality is beginningless, endless, devoid of all names and forms, beyond all speech and mind, the omnipotent whole which is absolutely changeless. It is like the waveless sea. It is absolutely self-realised and complete in Itself, and cannot be defined by any expressions such as 'this' or 'such'.[65]

Even the Narada Pancharatra, which is much more theistic than any other mentioned Samhitas, and which has come very much under the influence of the Bhagavata purana, could not keep out the Advaitic elements. It not only describes Brahman as attributeless, desireless and unattached,[66] or as one without a second,[67] or as the only all-pervading Reality,[68] but it also declares that Brahman alone is true, and that the whole world is false (mithya).[69]

The Vishnu Samhita is equally emphatic in declaring that the manifoldness is false. It gives the illustrations of mirrors and images, moon and its many reflections in water, and declares that only the ignorant perceives plurality. For a true seer the reality is one.[70] The same negation of duality is found in a more emphatic way in the Brahma Samhita.[71]

All the foregoing accounts leave us in no doubt about the predominantly Advaitic nature of the Pancharatra philosophy.

Immanent Aspect of the Supreme Being

The immanent aspect of the Supreme Being is inseparably bound up with the story of creation, and can, therefore, hardly be treated more conveniently than by taking the latter throughout as our starting point, yet for the sake of classified treatment we shall abstract the account of the immanent aspect from its cosmogonical context.

Lakshmi as Associated with the Supreme Being

The Supreme Being who is described as purely transcendent or 'wholly other', is, in Its immanent aspect, somehow, associated with a creative power (Shakti), a dynamic principle, which is spoken of figuratively as Its consort Lakshmi. Lakshmi is here not merely a consort of the Lord, but also a philosophical principle, a metaphysical complement of the Lord, Its creative potency. In the Samhitas the Supreme Being is not at all concerned with the creation etc., of the world. Lakshmi practically usurps the place of the Supreme Being in this respect. In her two aspects which are named as Bhuti and Kriya, she is the material as well as the instrumental cause of the world.

With the association of Lakshmi (who is said to be lying dormant in It before the start of creation) the Supreme Being passes from its undifferentiated and transcendent form to a personal form characterised bv six gunas, viz., jnana, aishvarya, shakti, bala, virya and tejas.[72] These gunas-aprakrta in nature-in their totality make up the body of Lakshmi and also of the immanent aspect of the Supreme Being named 'para', or sometimes as Vasudeva, who is referred to as 'shadgunyavigraham devam',[73] and who is the highest personal God. It should be noted here that these gunas are not associated with, and hence do not in any way affect, the 'Being' or the essence of the transcendent Supreme Being, because they are merely concerned with Its 'becoming' or manifestations. The transcendent Brahman and the immanent Lord Narayana who is associated with Lakshmi, are regarded as distinct in the[74] Lakshmi Tantra.

Why is Lakshmi Postulated?

For the Pancharatra thinkers the Ultimate Reality is the one, unmoving, unchanging, transcendent Brahman. But then the problem arose as to how to account for the changing world. How then does the infinite and perfect Brahman appear as the finite and imperfect world? This was the problem before Shankara as well. Shankara brought in the concept of Maya to relate the transcendent Brahman with the changing world. The Pancharatra thinkers also introduced the principle of shakti, manifestly with the same purpose. Both these principles are meant to supply the missing link between the transcendent Brahman and the immanent world.

It is interesting to note here that like the Maya of the Advaita, Shakti is also regarded as neither real nor unreal. It can neither be affirmed nor negated. It is neither shanta (unmanifest) nor udita (manifest) nor madhyama (middle position of the two).[75] The Pancharatra thinkers could not explain such a queer position. But perhaps what they meant was to say that it has subsistence (bhava) but not existence (satta). The difference between a subsistent and an existent can be made clear by the following example. When I say, 'I am in the room', 'I' exist, 'room' exists, but does 'in' exist? And yet it has a meaning, a connotation. In the same way Lakshmi subsists but does not exist. Perhaps the Pancharatra thinkers must have been hinting at the same when they said 'svarupe naiva drshyante drshyante karyatastu sa.'[76]

In the Lakshmi Tantra, Lakshmi describes herself as follows, "I am its supreme Shakti, Ahamta, eternal, unchanging. My activity is of the nature of desire to create. I create of my own independent power, by means of a myriad part of myself. I become two kinds of beings, the knower and the known, chitshakti being the enlightener of both."[77]

Lakshmi further describes herself as the creative aspect of the Lord.[78] The supreme Reality is unmoving and hence non-active. Whenever Brahman is described as cause, it should be understood that it refers to Lakshmi who acts in a manifold way for the welfare of the world in the forms of Samkarshana etc.[79]

Lakshmi and Brahman are said to be one only.[80] This is because they differ in connotation, and not in denotation. The Ahirbudhnya Samhita says that they stand in relation of 'shakti' and 'shaktimat' and therefore one cannot be conceived without the other.[81]

In the Lakshmi Tantra the mutual relation of the two is declared to be one of inseparable connection of inherence like that of an attribute and its bearer, subsistence and that which subsists, 'I' ness and 'I' etc. Their relation is regarded as identical because of their unbroken association (avinabhava) and samavaya (inherence).[82]

'Though this sort of distinction is maintained between Lakshmi and the Lord, and they do not completely coalesce, yet this dualism is, strictly speaking, a makeshift for preserving the transcendent nature of Brahman.[83]

Manifestations of the Supreme Being in its immanent aspect.

The central dogma of the Pancharatra religion is that the Deity manifests Himself in five-fold forms, viz., Para, Vyuha, Vibhava, Antaryamin and Archa.[84] Schrader suggests that this dogma is an attempt to interpret philosophically the Pancharatra sattra of Purusha Narayana spoken of in the Shatapatha Brahmana (iii. 6 i).[85] It, however, seems to be an attempt to bring the Supreme Transcendent One into living and loving touch with the mundane world.

Para Manifestation

The Para form is sometimes described as the first immanent manifestation of the Supreme Being. But sometimes it is said to have sprung from a still higher, the very first form of God.[86] This first form is referred to as 'the best of the purushas' and 'the Highest Light', seen by the Brahmanas in meditation.[87] This form is immanent only and should not be confused with the supreme transcendent one. This is clear when it is said that this form has originated from 'that which has all forms and no form', 'Brahman without beginning, middle and end'.

God as para is sometimes identified with and

sometimes distinguished from Vyuha Vasudeva. When the two are distinguished the Vyuha Vasudeva is said to have sprung from the para Vasudeva.[88]

The Padma Tantra describes para Vasudeva as dividing himself 'for some reason' and becoming with one half the Vyuha Vasudeva and with the other Narayana, the creator of the primeval waters. The para is adorned with nine chief ornaments and weapons, which symbolically represent the principles of the Universe.[89]

Vyuha Manifestation

The appearance of gunas in Lakshmi and Narayana denotes the beginning of the process of vyuha or emanation.[90] Vasudeva, characterised by the six gunas, is sometimes called the first vyuha. From Vasudeva emanates Samkarshana in whom jnana and bala alone get manifested. From Samkarshana comes Pradyumna to whom belong aishvarya and virya. From Pradyumna emanates Aniruddha to whom shakti and tejas appertain. This, however, does not mean that each vyuha has only two gunas, but each vyuha is Vasudeva himself with his six gunas, of which, however, only two in each case become manifest.[91] In the Lakshmi Tantra all these vyuhas are said to proceed from Lakshmi.[92] The Vihagendra Samhita, however, maintains that they come from Vasudeva[93].

As we have seen, the Pancharatra thinkers were very much particular in safeguarding and preserving the purity and unchanged nature of the transcendent

Supreme Being. From that point of view, the chief merit, and hence its primary significance, is that it is such a process of emanation in which the Supreme Being remains unaffected and unchanged in all the five-fold manifestations.

Avatara Manifestation

Closely connected with the doctrine of vyuhas, is the next manifestation of God, named as vibhava (Manifestation) or avatara (Descent). The only Supreme Being the Pancharatra philosophers knew about was the Transcendent One, who was not in any way directly related to the world. Therefore, the Samhitas explicitly describe the avataras as either all springing from Aniruddha,[94] or some from Vasudeva and the rest from the other three Vyuhas.[95] One should not be mistaken here in assuming that the Supreme Being Himself takes avatara. This is a pauranic conception. The Pancharatra Samhitas nowhere maintain that the Supreme Being, laying aside Its transcendent, unmoving nature assumes these finite forms. This is unpermissible by the premises of the system. The Supreme Being is merely a spectator with an attitude of passivity and indifference. It cherishes no attachment to the mundane world, and it is beyond Its nature to do so.[96]

Antaryamin Manifestation

The forth manifestation is the Antaryamin avatara, which is Aniruddha as the 'Inner Ruler' of all souls.[97] It is a mysterious power seated in the 'lotus of the heart'. Here again it should be noted that this is not a manifestation of the Supreme Being, but only of Aniruddha, one of the vyuhas.

Archa Manifestation

The Pancharatra Samhitas, unlike Narayaniya, finally recognise the archa manifestation of God. An inanimate object (i. e. image of Vishnu), if duly consecrated according to the Pancharatra rites, acquires a miraculous power, and the Shakti of Vishnu descends into it. It is meant for the purpose of daily worship.[98]

This archa worship is different from the pratima worship. In the latter the symbol is the locus, on which the devotee concentrates his thought. But no sooner the thought is centralised, than the locus soon gets out of his vision and no necessity thereof is felt. But in the archa worship, on the other hand, the devotee feels the very presence of God in it. And as such the inanimate image soon acquires a new meaning, becomes the object of love, of heart's hankering and of eye's rest. This we find in the religion of the Alvars as well, who are the Tamil Vaishnava saints.

Appraisal

The pancharatra thinkers accept one Supreme Reality which is unambiguously declared to be an impersonal homogeneous mass of pure consciousness transcending all attributes. To It are attributed almost all those negative epithets with which the

Upanishads describe the acosmic form of the Ultimate Reality. They start with that concept of the Ultimate Reality in which there is no inwardness or outwardness, coming in or going out, but there is a stillness and sameness everywhere. But as they cannot remain satisfied with this unhappy position which fails to gratify fully their religious fervour, they are forced to introduce the dynamic concept in some other way. Thus their religious instinct leads them to draw a distinction between the trancendental and the empirical Realities by creating a dichotomy in the Reality Itself.

However, it should be noted that the transcendent impersonal Reality alone appears as personal empirical Reality or God, through Its association with maya (Narayaniya view) or with Shakti (Samhita view). This personal form is said to be assumed for the purposes of devotion and worship (Narayaniya view) or for the purposes of creation (Samhita view). It has meaning only for the empirical or religious consciousness and not for the philosophical insight.

The Pancharatra thinkers deny self-revelation to the transcendent Supreme Being. For them nothing perfect, nothing genuinely real can move. Only the personal God can reveal Himself. The demand for Godhead is a demand of the practical reason. All the impulses and feelings of religion, though lofty and noble, belong to the lower plane of empirical consciousness and have no place in the transcendent Reality. In this way the God of religion is less than the Absolute of philosophy and has no meaning outside the religious or empirical consciousness. The Absolute is not God because It is related to nothing and there cannot be a practical relation between It and the world. So the conclusion that follows from this is that the personal form is not the highest reality but the highest appearance and therefore must suffer the transforming plunge into the ultimate transcendent One. The personal form is the first in the emanation series, a fact which confirms that it is something not ultimately real and hence may at any moment be withdrawn into the Absolute.

This conclusion seems to be quite inevitable in the Pancharatra philosophy. After declaring God of religion (i.e. Vasudeva) as a later appearance and hence a Reality of a lower order, the Pancharatra School has no choice but to accept this ultimate unreality. Such a conclusion would be unpalatable to a Vishishtadvaitin, but no other conclusion can legitimately be drawn from this.

The Pancharatra thinkers are led to believe in the personal God because of their religious instinct, but such a God who has no reality of His own, whose existence depends on other principles (Viz. the Supreme Being and the Shakti), cannot satisfy religious aspirations. The religious consciousness cannot be content with worshipping a God who is discovered not to be supreme at all, but to be an appearance of a more Ultimate Being. Further we are faced with the problem of the ontological status of God.

Does He really exist anywhere in the world? Has He a being for Himself as well as an appearance for others? The other difficulty that crops up here and which we have discussed in the next chapter is with regard to the relation of the Shakti to the Supreme Being.

The Pancharatra thinkers do not emphasise the mayavada of the Advaita Vedanta, but their predominantly transcendent Absolute seems to be a denial of the plurality of the immanent world. Indeed the Absolute has been made so much transcendent that one may conceive the continuity of immanent life side by side with the trancendent Absolute. Though the immanent life runs side by side with the transcendent Being, in the silence of the transcendent Being the immanent life has no place. From some of the extremely advaitic utterances of the Samhitas one can be led to think that the Absolute is the only reality and the immanent life has no reality at all. In fact such a conclusion is against the spirit of the practical Pancharatra, but this alone is its legitimate theoretical position.

The Pancharatra thinkers not only emphasise the absolute and transcendent nature of the Supreme Being, but also regard It as a Being self-centred and self-contented, so much so that It is not in the least concerned with the mundane world. In their eagerness to preserve and emphasise the purity, perfection and transcendent nature of Brahman, they come to the view that it is not the Supreme Being who is responsible for the creation etc. of the world. Not only does It not create the world, but also remains quite unaffected by the changes which are necessary to bring about the world. Like the Advaitins the Pancharatra thinkers emphasise the transcendence of God so much that they forget entirely its immanent aspect. In order to preserve the divine transcendence and perfection which seem incompatible with Its being an active agent in relation to the world they posit a series of emanations and introduce mediating principles like Shakti, Vyuhas, Brahma etc. But they never equate the Supreme Being with these emanations and intermediaries, either individually or taken together. It is not the Supreme Being who assumes these forms. They rather emanate from It and the speciality of this process of emanation is that in it while bringing the product into existence, the source of the product remains unchanged. The Supreme Being is the unchanging one who though unchanging is the basis of all changes. In this respect the Supreme Being of the Pancharatra school comes nearer to the concept of an 'absentee Deity' or 'slumbering God'. It has been aptly described in the Samhitas as 'windless atmosphere' or 'motionless sea'. To speak of such a waveless state and a quietness in the Absolute and also its trascendent changeless nature which remains intact even in the process of creation, resembles the absolutistic position of the Advaitins.

But the very transcendence of the Supreme Being

signifies an artificial relation with the world. Such an Absolute 'wholly other' with whom we can maintain no relations and from whom we can cherish no hopes cannot satisfy any human aspiration. In being sheer transcendent It hopelessly falls short of our expectations. A Supreme Being who has no unfulfilled purposes, no unsolved problems, who need not wait upon us and who cannot enter into reciprocal intercourse with the finite spirits cannot be speculatively satisfying. It leaves unanswered a fundamental problem as to why the Absolute which is eternally perfect, to whom there is nothing unaccomplished should instruct, as it were, the Shakti or Brahma to create the universe. Further, in what relation does the so-called unrelated Absolute stand to that Universe? Both cannot be real, otherwise we shall have to give some place to the imperfect world in the perfect Absolute.

The fundamental defect with these thinkers is that they start with a static, inert and empty Absolute arrived at by a kind of via negativa and through it they try to explain the world. The most fruitful method is to start with the concrete world of experience and to transfer to the Absolute the most significant and revealing features of the world. The Absolute then comes to be a system of relations, a system in which every element of experience has a place and meaning, not in its coarse but transmuted form.

References and foot notes

1. एतत्त्वया नविज्ञेयं रूपवानिति दृश्यते ।
माया ह्येषा मया सृष्टा यन्मां पश्यसि नारद ॥ 340. 44-5

2. Ibid 339. 4.
cf. सर्वोपमानरहितं वागतीतं स्ववेदनम् ।
अस्तीति परमं वस्तुं निरालम्बमतीन्द्रियम् Jayakhya V. 29

3. न दृश्यः चक्षुषा योऽसौ न स्पृश्यः स्पर्शनेन च ।
न घ्रेयश्चैव गन्धेन रसेन च विवर्जितः । 340. 21

4. स्वसंवेद्यं तु तद्विद्धि गन्धः पुष्पादिगो यथा ।
Jayakhya IV. 76

5. यस्य प्रसादं कुरुते सर्वंतं द्रष्टुमर्हति । 337. 19.
cf. Katha & Mundaka upanishads

6. 340. 1.

7. 337. 12.

8. See Supra F. N. 5.

9. न सः शक्यस्त्वभंक्तेन द्रष्टुं देवः कथंचन । 337. 53

10. 337. 53.

11. Shariraka bhashya I. 2.14 ; also Bhajagovindam

12. (अ) तत्र यः परमात्मा हि नित्यं निर्गुणः स्मृतः ।
स हि नारायणो ज्ञेयः सर्वात्मा पुरुषो हि सः ॥ 352. 14

(आ) महापुरुष शब्दं विभर्त्येकः सनातनः । 352. 9

(इ) ईश्वरो हि जगत्स्रष्टा प्रभु नारायणो विराट् । 348-12

13. अजो नित्यः शाश्वतश्च निर्गुणो निष्कलस्तथा । 340-23

14. यत्तत्सूक्ष्मविज्ञेयमव्यक्तमचलं ध्रुवम् ।
इन्द्रियैरिन्द्रयार्थैश्च सर्वभूतैश्च वर्जितम् ॥ 335-29

15. (अ) यश्च सर्वगतः साक्षी लोकस्यात्मेति कथ्यते । 340. 22
(आ) सर्वेषां साक्षिभूतो असौ न ग्राह्यो केनचिद् क्वचिद् ॥ 352. 4.
Compare the concept of अन्तर्यामी of the बृहदारण्यक उपनिषद with these two passages taken together.

16. एको हुताशो बहुधा समिध्यते एकः सूर्यस्तपसोयोनिरेका ॥
एको वायु र्बहुधा वाति लोके महोदधिश्चांभसां योनिरेकः ॥
पुरुषश्चैको निर्गुणो विश्वरूपस्तं निर्गुणं पुरुषं चाविशंति ।
हित्वा गुणमयं सर्वं कर्म हित्वा शुभाशुभम् ।
उभे सत्यानृते त्यक्त्वा एवं भवति निर्गुणः ॥
यत्तत्कृत्स्नं लोकतन्त्रस्य धामवेद्यं परं बोधनीयं स बोद्धा ।
मन्ता मन्तव्यं प्राशिता प्राशनीयं घ्राता घ्रेयं स्पर्शिता स्पर्शनीयं
द्रष्टा द्रष्टव्यं श्राविता श्रावणीयं ज्ञाता ज्ञेयं सगुणं निर्गुणं च ॥
352. 9 to 18

17. अशरीरः शरीरेषु सर्वेषु निवसत्यसौ । 352-3

18. (अ) निर्गुणो गुणभुक् चैव गुणस्रष्टा गुणाधिकः । 340. 28
(आ) 'निर्गुणायगुणात्मने' 389-3
(इ) 'सगुणो निर्गुणोऽपि च' 348. 13, 352. 18

19. (अ) सत्वं रजस्तमश्चैव न गुणास्तं भजन्ति वै । 340-22
(आ) त्रिगुण व्यतिरिक्तो (335. 30)

20. 'निष्क्रियः' 340. 43,

21. (अ) 'जगत्स्रष्टा' 348-12
(आ) मत्तः सर्वं संभवति जगत् स्थावरं जंगमम् ।
अक्षरं च क्षरं चैव सच्चासच्चैव नारद ॥ 340-42

22. 339-4

23. 340-43
24. 340-69
25. 337-61,62
26. 339-1
27. 339-4
28. 339-4 ; 344-53,54
29. 339-4
30. 342-39
31. 347-17
32. 345-6
33. 339-4
34. 339-4
35. 340-42
36. 339-4 ; 340-26,42
37. 342-25
38. 343-25
39. 343-75
40. 343-89
41. 342-2 ; 344-16,17
42. 344-16,17
43. 340-3,6

44. The word Vyuha (vi + uha = shoving as under) denotes that peculiar process of creation, which while bringing the product into existence leaves the source of the product unchanged. (Kashmira Shaivism-J. C. Chatterjee p. 59). The word Vyuha further indicates that out of the six attributes of Vasudeva

(see our Samhita account and Lakshmi Tantra V. 21), which break up into three pairs of two attributes, each of the three Vyuhas emanates one by one. The word Vyuha further suggests that each one of the three, except the first, emanates from the anterior one, like one flame proceding from another flame. (Padmatantra I. 2.21)

The origin of this doctrine may, perhaps, be found in the worship of Vasudeva and Samkarshana. Strictly speaking the Vyuhas are three only, but sometimes Vasudeva is also included and the number comes to four. These four subordinate manifestations of the Supreme Deity may very well be compared with (and it is not improbable that they might have been thought after the analogy of) Prajna, Virata, Vishva and Taijasa in the Advaita Vedanta.

All the four Vyuhas have not always been recognised in this cult. The Narayaniya (349-57) clearly says so and this is attested by the inscriptions. The Ghoshundi and Nanaghata inscriptions mention only two forms, Vasudeva and Samkarshana. This suggests that originally only two Vyuhas were recognised, and afterwards [(either on the above mentioned analogy with the Advaita or, as Schrader suggests, to bring the original non-brahminic Pancharatra into agreement with the Veda and the famous saying of the Purusha Sukta (fourth stanza) about the four quarters of God, (See our introduction for the non-brahminic origin of the Pancharatra)] two more members of the family of Krishna, viz., his son and grandson, were deified. The employment of this geneological series may either be due to enable the untutored people to grasp the idea of the rather difficult series of emanation of the Samkhya system, or it may be a theologism created to give Vasudeva etc., a permanent place in the teachings and worship of the Pancharatra Community (see Epigraphica Indica XVI. P. 25 for the two inscriptions, and Introduction to the Pancharatra and Ahirbudhnya Samhita-pp. 144, 145, for Schrader's suggestion; and Archeological Survey of Western India pp. 60).

The doctrine of Vyuha does not occur in the vedic literature; nor do we find it in the Gita. The Gita (VII.4-5) however mentions, as Prakritis of Vasudeva five elements, mind, buddhi, egoism and jiva. But we do not find any evidence for R. G. Bhandarkar's conjecture that these elements were later on personified into Samkarshana, Pradyumna and Aniruddha.

The Vyuha doctrine in its characteristic form does not occur in the Puranas as well. In the Vishnu Purana the names of the four Vyuhas appear only as the names of Krishna and the members of his family (Chapt. V). They occur in the same way in the Bhagavata Purana-(Chapt. X). But often in this Purana the Deity is greeted as having four forms-Vasudeva, Samkarshana, Pradyumna and Aniruddha-but what the Deity is, or does, under those forms is not elaborated except in one passage (IV. 24) where Vasudeva is equated with the Transcendent (Para), Samkarshana with the Subtle (Sukshma), Pradyumna with the understanding (Buddhi) and Aniruddha with Mind (Manas) (cf. I. 5 ; VI. 16 ; X. 40 ; XI. 15 ; XII. 11). In the Markandeya and Kurma Puranas Narayana is said to manifest Himself in four forms, which correspond to the four Vyuhas. All these Puranas, however, betray the influence of the Narayaniya and not of the later Pancharatra Samhitas.

For Sankara's and Ramanuja's treatment of the Vyuha doctrine see my paper 'Does Badarayana favour Pancharatra ?', Philosophical Quarterly, April 1965.

45. यो वासुदेवो भगवान्क्षेत्रज्ञो निर्गुणात्मकः ।
ज्ञेयः स एव राजेन्द्र जीवः संकर्षणः प्रभुः ॥
संकर्षणाच्च प्रद्युम्नाद् मनोभूतः स उच्यते ।
प्रद्युम्नाद्योऽनिरुद्धस्तु सोऽहंकार स ईश्वरः ॥ 340. 40-41.

46. See my paper Loc. cit.

47. 340-74 ff.

48. यथा ह्यसि त्वमव्यक्तो ह्यमूर्तो मूर्ततां गतः ।
Jayakhya Samhita IV.20.

49. (अ) अनादि तदनन्तं च न सत्तन्नासदुच्यते । Ibid IV.63.
(आ) नैव भावो न चाभावस्तद्भावार्चितये न च ।
Ahirbudhnya II. 50.

50. (अ) वर्तमानं न तद्ब्रह्म नातीतं नैव भावि तत् । Ibid II.47.
(आ) अनंतो देशकालादि परिच्छेदविवर्जितः ।
Lakshmi Tantra II. 8.
See Parama Prakasha I. 3.43 and 55 as well

51. अनाद्यन्तं परं ब्रह्म यत्तदक्षरमव्ययम् ।
अनामरूपसंवेद्यमवाङ्मनसगोचरम् ॥ Ahirbudhnya II. 6.

52. अग्रतः पृष्ठतो नैव नोर्ध्वतः पार्श्वयोः द्वयोः ।
न दीर्घं नैव च ह्रस्वं न स्थूलं नैव चाप्यणु । Ibid II.47-49

53. (अ) सर्वद्वन्द्वविनिर्मुक्तं सर्वोपाधिविवर्जितम् । Ibid II.53
(आ) सर्वोपमानरहितं वागतीतं स्ववेदनम् ।
अस्तीति परमं वस्तु निरालम्बमतीन्द्रियम् ।। Jayakhya V.29
(इ) स्वसंवेद्यमनौपम्यं पराकाष्ठा परागतिः । Ibid IV. 61.

54. (अ) सर्वतः शांत एवासौ निर्विकारः सनातनः ।
Lakshmi Tantra II. 8.
(आ) निस्तरंगामृताम्भोधिकल्पम् । Ibid II.10.
(इ) निरवद्यमविक्षिप्तमतरंगार्णवोपमम् ।
Ahirbudhnya II.23.
(ई) 'सर्वक्रियाविनिर्मुक्तम्' Jayakhya. IV.61.

55. (अ) 'सर्वेषामाश्रयः प्रभुः' Ibid. IV. 61
(आ) 'सर्वकारणकारणम्' Ahirbudhnya. II. 53.
(इ) आत्मन्यानंद संस्थस्य Jayakhya. V. 30.

56. (अ) ज्ञानमेव परं रूपं ब्रह्मणः परमात्मनः ।
Ahirbudhnya. II. 62.
(आ) 'ज्ञानाय निस्तरंगाय' Lakshmi Tantra. I. 1.
(इ) आनंदं लक्षणं ब्रह्म सर्वं हेय विवर्जितम् ।
Jayakhya. IV. 60.
(ई) 'अप्राकृत गुण स्पर्शम्' Ahirbudhnya. II. 24.
(उ) 'निर्गुणो गुणभोक्ता च' Jayakhya. II. 65.

57. (अ) यत्सर्वव्यापकं देवं परमं ब्रह्म शाश्वतम् । Ibid. IV. 2.
(आ) सर्वभूतकृतावासं सर्वं व्याप्य व्यवस्थितम् ।
Ahirbudhnya. II. 23.

58. I. V. 29-34.

59. Ibid. I. VI. 40

60. II. 1-10

61. एवमेकः परो देवो नानाशक्त्यात्मरूपधृत् ।
नारायणः परं ब्रह्म निष्ठासन्ब्रह्मवेदिनाम् ।। IV. 116-117
also IV. 111-115

62. अयः पिंडे यथा वह्निर्भिन्नस्तिष्ठत्यभिन्नवत् ।
तद्वत् सर्वमिदं देवो व्यावृत्य परितिष्ठति ।।
निर्मलेदर्पणे यद्वत् किञ्चिद् वस्त्वभितिष्ठति ।
न च दर्पणस्यास्ति अस्ति तस्य च तद् द्विज ।।
अस्मिन्मायामये विश्वे व्यापी सर्वेश्वरः प्रभुः ।
सर्वदा विद्धि असक्तश्च यथाऽम्भः पुष्करच्छदे ।। IV. 83-86

63. घटसंस्थं यथाऽऽकाशं नीयमानं विभाव्यते ।
नाकाशं कुत्रचिद्याति नयनात्तु घटस्य च ।।
चलाचलत्वमेवं हि विभोश्चैवानुमीयते ।
आकाशः संचयो वायुस्तद् द्वयोरप्यभेदता ।
तथा तस्याविभक्त्यैक्यं भूतानां हि परस्य च ।। IV. 88, 89, 92.

64. स एव भगवान्देवः परमात्मा जगद् गुरुः ।
देवतादि विभागेन विभिन्नो व्यवतिष्ठते ।।
यथैव भिन्न वर्णानां द्रव्याणामाश्रये सति ।
स्फाटिकस्य मणे रूपमन्यच्चान्यच्च लक्ष्यते ।।
तथा गुणमयैर्भावैरेको हि पुरुषः परः ।
भिन्नरूपो जगत्यस्मिन् बद्धो मुक्तश्च जायते ।। II. 87-90

65. See Chapter III

66. निर्गुणं निरीहं च निर्लिप्तमीश्वरं भजे । I. 5.6

67. 'एकोऽयं न द्वितीयश्च' II. 3.19

68. एकैवेश्वरः शश्वद्विश्वेषु निखिलेषुच । II. 1.22

69. ब्रह्मादि स्तम्बपर्यन्तं सर्वं मिथ्यैव नारद ।
भज सत्यं परं ब्रह्मं राधेशं त्रिगुणात्परम् ॥ II. 2-100

70. दर्पणानां बहुत्वे तु दृश्यन्ते नैकधा यथा ।
तद्वत् बहुत्वं मन्यन्ते विष्णोस्तस्याल्पचेतसः ॥
यथाऽम्भसीन्दुबिम्बानि प्रतिशब्दाश्च नैकधा ।
एकोऽप्यात्मा बहुष्वेवमित्याहुस्तत्त्वदर्शिनः ॥
सहि आत्मान्तरात्मा च परमात्मा च स स्मृतः ।

71. द्वैतं नास्तीति बोधेन मनसो द्वैतनाशनम् ।
ब्रह्मविद् भवति ब्रह्म इत्येषा च परा श्रुतिः ॥

72. See the details in the Chapter III

73. निर्गुणोपि गुणानेतानधिष्ठायात्मवाञ्छया ।
Lakshmi Tantra III. 9. 'also II. 27-35 ; VI. 25

74. भगवान्नारायणो देवो भावो लक्ष्मीरहं परा ।
लक्ष्मीनारायणाख्यातमतो ब्रह्म सनातनम् ॥ Ibid II. 15

75. (अ) इदंतया विधातुं सा न निषेद्धुं च शक्यते ।
(आ) न शान्ता नोदिता नापि मध्यमाहं चिदात्मिका । Ibid IV. 2

76. Ahirbudhnya III. 2

77. (अ) 'भावोऽहं तादृशो हरेः' Lakshmi Tantra IV. 1
(आ) तस्य या परमा शक्ति ज्योत्स्नेव हिमदीधितेः ।
सर्वावस्थागता देवी स्वात्मभूतानपायिनी ॥
अहं नारायणी शक्तिः सिसृक्षा लक्षणा तदा ।
अहं नारायणी शक्तिः सुषुप्सा लक्षणा हि सा ॥
Lakshmi Tantra II. 11, 12
(इ) ईशो नारायणो ज्ञेयः ईशता तस्य चाप्यहम् ।
ईशितव्यं तु विज्ञेयं चिदचिच्च पुरंदर ॥ Ibid III. 14

(ई) विभक्ते अपि ते एते शक्ती चिदचिदात्मके ।
मत्स्वाच्छन्द्य वशेनैव मम रूपे सनातने ॥ Ibid III. 25
See XIV. 1-4 and II. 22-23 as well

78. (अ) व्यापारस्तस्य देवस्य साऽहमस्मि न संशयः ।
मयाकृतं हि यत्कर्म तेन तत्कृतमुच्यते ॥
अहं हि तस्य देवस्य स्मृता व्याप्रियमाणता । Ibid XI. 6-7

(आ) जगत्प्रकृतिभावो में यः सा शक्तिरितीर्यते । Ibid II. 29

79. नटः प्रवर्तते यद्वत् वेषचेष्टाभेदवान् ।
तद्वत् एकापि सैवाहं ज्ञानशक्त्यादिभिः गुणैः ॥
संकर्षणादि सद्भावं भजे लोकहितेप्सया ॥ Ibid II. 55-56
cf. Ahirbudhnya IX. 46

80. 'तौ इमौ एकधा एव उक्तौ' Ahirbudhnya VI. 2

81. नैव शक्त्या विना कश्चिच्छक्तिमानस्ति कारणम् ।
न च शक्तिमता शक्तिविनैका व्यवतिष्ठते ॥ Ibid VI. 3

82. (अ) अहमर्थसमुत्था च साहंता परिकीर्तिता ।
अन्योन्येनाविनाभावादन्योन्येन समन्वयात् ॥
तादात्म्यं विद्धि सम्बन्धं मम नाथस्योभयोः ।।
अहंतया विनाहं हि निरुपाख्यो न सिध्यति ।
अहमर्थं विनाहंता निराधारा न सिध्यति ॥
Lakshmi Tantra II. 17-19

(आ) विष्णोः सर्वांगं सम्पूर्णा भावाभावानुगामिनी ।
शक्ति नारायणी दिव्या सर्वसिद्धान्त सम्मता ॥
देवाच्छक्तिमतो भिन्ना ब्रह्मणः परमेष्ठिनः ।
एष च एषा च शास्त्रेषु धर्म धर्मि स्वभावतः ॥
भवद्भाव स्वरूपेण तत्त्वमेकमिवोदितौ ।
Ahirbudhnya III. 24-26

83. See Schrader, Loc. cit. P. 30

84. मम प्रकाराः पञ्चेति प्राहुः वेदान्तपारगाः ।

Vishvakshena Samhita P. 122

85. See Schrader, Loc. cit. P. 325 for details.

86. (अ) 'रूपमाद्यं सनातनम्' Padma Tantra I.1.
(आ) 'वासुदेवाह्वयं महः, Vishnu Tilaka II. 10
(इ) 'महः परं भास्वरम्' Ahirbudhnya XLIII.

87. Padma Tantra I. 3.16 ff

88. पुरुषात्वासुदेवोऽभूत चत्वारोह्यभवन्स्ततः ।

Parama Prakasha I. 2.3

cf. Padma Tantra first Pada, Second adhyaya.

89. Vishnu Tilaka II. 29 ff.; Schradnr, Loc. cit., P. 52.

90. See Supra foot note 73.

91. See Supra foot note 44, and infra chapter.III.

92. II. 27-35.

93. 'भूतानां बीजमव्ययम्' II. 15

94. Lakshmi Tantra II. 55.

95. Padma Tantra I. 2.81. ff

96. The Ahirbudhnya Samhita mentions thirtynine principal avataras (V. 50 ff.; cf. Sattavata Samhita V. 57-66). See for forms, Shaktis, colours and kinds of avataras, Sattvata Samhita chapters III, IV and V; and Schrader, Loc. cit., PP. 42-48.

97. 'नियन्ता सर्वं देहीनाम्'

Vishvakshena Samhita P. 122.

CHAPTER III

THE NATURE OF THE WORLD

Introduction

The history of philosophy reveals a constant recurrence of some fundamental problems. One of such problems is 'How has the world come to exist ?' The earliest philosophic view as regards the nature of the Supreme Being appears to have arisen out of an attempt to answer this problem. The same problem found expression in the Vishvakarma hymns of the Rigveda (X. 81.4). The intricacy and insolubility of the problem led the author of the Nasadiya Sukta to admit his defeat when he exclaimed "who can know the origin of this world? It is also doubtful whether the very supervisor of this world in the highest heaven knows it or not ! " (Rigveda X. 129.6.7).

Of all the problems that attracted the attention of the Pancharatra thinkers, it was this that interested them most. Speculating on cosmological problems. and propounding elaborate cosmological theories and doctrines seem to have been a favourite topic for them. All the Pancharatra doctrines-Philosophical as well as Theological - are set in their cosmogonic context. It will not therefore be too much to say that the philosophy of these thinkers begins with the story of creation.

Ontological status of the world

The problem of the ontological status of the world has not been given due consideration by the Pancharatra thinkers. This is because their interest is centred round another cosmological problem-viz., how should the changing world be related to the changeless Brahman-and therefore they do not bother much about any other cosmological problem. From the account of the nature of the Ultimate Reality it follows that with regard to the ontological status of the world the attitude of the Pancharatra thinkers was pseudo-realistic. Apparently they seem to regard the world as real, but from the premisses of the system it is evident that the reality can be phenomenal only. Though many of the Samhitas are indifferent to the Advaitic doctrine of Maya in some of them this doctrine has found a distinct expression.[1]

The world as emanation

The basic cosmological problem before the Pancharatra thinkers is, 'How can the imperfect world arise out of a perfect Being?' It is indisputable that the universe is full of imperfections, that the Supreme Being is perfect and that the world issues out of the Supreme Being. But trouble arises when it is asked whether the Supreme Being can be regarded as an active agent in relation to the world, which is quite different from It in nature, and yet remains unaffected by the changes necessary to bring about the world. Can the Supreme Being, the changeless, be regarded as the basis and the *raison d' etre* of the changing world ? Will not Its perfect nature be hampered if It is conceived to be directly related to an imperfect world ?

The Pancharatra thinkers deny the possibility of the Supreme Being being an active agent of, and directly related to, the world. The transcendent, perfect and the unchanging Supreme Being is so far removed in character from the changing imperfect world that not only is It regarded as incapable of being described as the cause of the world, but It is also thought to be incapable of being actively or directly related to it. Consequently they take great pains to show how the changing world springs from and is related to the unchanging Supreme Being. In order to account for this they postulate various intermediaries between the Supreme Being and the world. The world is regarded as springing or emanating not directly from the Supreme Being but from Its Shakti, named Lakshmi, which, described as an aspect of the Supreme Being, is so eternally distinct from Its nature that though engaged in creation etc., it leaves the essential nature of the Supreme Being unaffected. The special contribution of the Pancharatra school is the theory of emanation (Vyuha-vada) which, while bringing the varying world into existence from the Supreme Being, leaves the latter quite unaffected. The doctrine of five-fold manifestations of the Deity, which is a central dogma of this school, is an outcome of this doctrine. Thus the world is regarded as an emanation from the Shakti of the Supreme Being and the Supreme Being is in no way concerned with it, save with the Shakti.

The cosmological account of the Narayaniya

The Narayaniya regards the Supreme Being as the creator of the world[3] but at the same time qualifies this by introducing a mythological account that the Supreme Being Itself does not do this work but commissions Brahma, who spontaneously rises out of It, to create and superintend the world.[3] Brahma is said to have obtained from the Supreme Being the intelligence necessary for this task.[4] Having unveiled to the creator of the cosmos the objects that are to be evolved, the Supreme Being is reported to have vanished in Its native form (mulam prakritim) and to have adopted the course of nivritti[5] or Yogic Sleep[6] (yoga nidra).

The Narayaniya holds that the process of creation starts in two parallel orders from two categories of matter and spirit which originate simultaneously from the Supreme Being. The first is a physical order of material causation and the second is a psychical order of conditioned existences named as Vyuhas.
The two orders are as follows :

1. Kshetrajna - prakriti - manas - ahamkara - gunas and mahabhutas.
2. Vasudeva - Samkarshana - Pradyumna - Aniruddha - Brahma.

In this way the Supreme Being Itself does not create but undergoes a series of emanations till Brahma, the creator, appears. The reason why the Supreme Being commissions Brahma and does not create Itself is, as we have said above, the desire of the Pancharatra thinkers to preserve the divine transcendence and perfection which seem incompatible with Its being an active agent in relation to the world.

The cosmological account of the Samhitas

The Samhitas propound an elaborate and complicated process of creation with the characteristic doctrines of three stages and six koshas of creation.

The only Ultimate Reality the Samhita thinkers recognise is the transcendent Supreme Being.[7] It dwells for timeless ages in Its transcendent form in a state of quietness which is compared to 'windless atmosphere' or 'motionless sea'. It suddenly stirs up and a resolve flashes up in It to start the process of creation. This resolve is attributed not to the Supreme Being but to Its Shakti - the creative potency which is spoken of figuratively as Its consort, Lakshmi. The Shakti of the Supreme Being, which was so far indistinguishable from It, existing only as it were in the form of 'darkness' or 'emptiness', opens her eyes and starts the process of creation with an infinite part of herself, in her dual aspect of Kriya (acting) and Bhuti (becoming). In the whole process of creation the Supreme Being, because of Its transcendent nature, remains so completely in the background that we are concerned only with the Shakti which as Bhuti appears as the universe, and as Kriya vitalises and governs it.[8] The Samhitas enumerate three stages and six koshas through which the world passes before it acquires its present gross imperfect form. The three stages are Shuddha Sarga, Mishra Sarga (Shuddhashuddha) and Sthula Sarga (Ashuddha). The six koshas appear distributively in the three stages. The first Kosha, named as Shakti Kosha, comprises of the Vyuhas and their Shaktis. The second is the Maya Kosha consisting of the Maya Shakti. The third Kosha is Prasuti Kosha in which Manus take birth. The fourth Kosha is Prakriti Kosha from which the Lotus, producing the cosmic egg, originates. The non-manifest and the manifest stages of the cosmic egg, named as Brahmanda Kosha and Jivadeha Kosha, are the fifth and the six koshas.[9]

In the first stage Lakshmi, Vasudeva with his six gunas, three vyuhas with their Shaktis, Vibhavas and Divine abode with all its inhabitants and paraphernalia appear. Under the second stage kutastha purusha and Maya Shakti, consisting of Niyati, Kala and Guna-body, evolve. The last stage is divided into two - primary and secondary. The primary level is on the pattern of the Samkhya system with some elaboration and modification. The secondary level consists of the cosmic egg and Brahma and it is the latter who creates the gross world that we perceive. Though there are many divergences as regards the details in different Samhitas the main stages in the evolution of the world from the Supreme Being are fairly represented in the above account.[10] All these cosmological details are the original contribution and distinctive feature of the Pancharatra school.

The impact of the Samkhya system on the Pancharatra

The Pancharatra thinkers display great keenness in pointing out the various stages through which the world passes before it acquires its present state. In formulating the details regarding the process of these stages specially at the primary level of the Ashuddha Sarga they betray the impact of the Samkhya with some important differences. Apparently they seem to deny the dualism of the Samkhya by accepting the subordination of the creative potency to the Supreme Being. But somehow this monism could not become thorough-going, because on the pattern of the Purushas of the Samkhya they regard the Supreme Being as purely transcendent and thus leave the cosmic evolution alone to the Shakti.

The Pancharatra cosmology compared with the Advaitic cosmology

The Pancharatra cosmology has very much in common with that of the Advaita. Both the schools deny the possibility of the Supreme Being, conceived as unchanging, being an active agent of, and directly related to, the world. Shankara ushers in the concept of Maya with the only purpose of relating the unchanging Brahman with the changing universe, and the principle of Shakti is introduced by the Pancharatra thinkers manifestly with the same purpose. Both these principles are pressed into service in order to supply the missing link between the transcendent Brahman and the immanent world. Shankara and the Pancharatra thinkers are so desperately eager to safeguard the purity, perfection and unchanged nature of the Supreme Being that they emphasise its transcendence at the cost of the reality of the world.

It is this eagerness which restrains them from regarding It as immanent in the world or as directly related to the world.

This position forces both the schools to postulate three other corollaries. Firstly, both the schools are led to postulate the highest personal God, who is the immanent appearance of the transcendent Supreme Being. The Ishvara of the Advaita and the Vasudeva of the Pancharatra serve only this purpose. Both of these are equally phenomenal, and the only difference between them is that the Ishvara of the Advaita is associated with Maya whereas the Vasudeva of the Pancharatra is associated with Lakshmi who is conceived in a more positive and determinate way than the Maya of the Advaita

Secondly, in both the Schools intermediaries (Hiranyagarbha, Virat etc. in the Advaita, and Vyuhas, Brahma etc. in the Pancharatra) are postulated between the transcendent Supreme and the immanent world so that the perfect nature of the Supreme can remain unimpaired.

Lastly, the Advaitic doctrine of Vivartavada and the Pancharatra doctrine of Vyuhavada are very similar. In both the doctrines, though the Supreme Being is regarded as the basis of the world, It is saved from being affected by the mutations of the world. It is not clear whether all the Pancharatra thinkers genuinely believe in the Satkarana-vada and the consequent view of the illusory manifestation

5

of the phenomenal world, but from the premises of the School one must legitimately expect them to do so.

Appraisal of the Pancharatra cosmology

The Pancharatra thinkers are quite emphatic in maintaining that the Supreme Being alone is the basis of the world, but they are equally emphatic in saying that It is quite unaffected by the changes which are necessary to bring about the world. It is the unchanging one who though unchanging is the explanation of all change. The desire of the Pancharatra thinkers to preserve the purity, perfection and the unchanging nature of the Supreme Being in relation to the changing world leads the Pancharatra thinkers to postulate the concept of Lakshmi, the doctrine of five-fold manifestations of God, and the various stages through which the evolution of the world takes place. However this way of overcoming the difficulty, though seemingly satisfactory, is really no solution to the problem at all. In so far as these mediating principles are regarded as distinct from the Supreme Being, they serve to bridge the gulf between It and the world' but when it is realised that they cannot be so regarded because then the problem arises of explaining the relation of the Supreme Being to these, they are immediately declared to be none other than the Supreme Being in one or the other of Its aspects.

The Pancharatra thinkers draw a distinction between the transcendence of divine consciousness and the immanence of Divine will which is represented by Shakti. The Supreme Being—which is said to consist of the consciousness-aspect—does not create the world, but simply expresses a 'will' and Shakti starts the process of creation. But why the Supreme Being so expresses a 'will' and why having once motivated the Shakti to create the world It no longer takes interest in it, are problems which they have left unanswered.

The Pancharatra thinkers seem to take a realistic attitude towards the universe, but their realism strictly interpreted, is only apparent. The transcendent nature of the Supreme Being is regarded by them as incompatible with the changing world and this gives rise to the view that the Supreme Being Itself is not responsible for the creation etc. of the world. This work is assigned to Shakti who therefore practically usurps the place of the Supreme Being in relation to the world. If the Supreme Being were the only reality and if It does not Stand related to the changing world, the only conclusion that logically follows is that the Supreme Being alone is real and the world is not real but only phenomenal. But this is quite a precarious and disturbing position for them and in order to avoid getting into it, they try to maintain that the Shakti is an aspect of the Supreme Being. But this position would have affected the transcendent and unchanging character of the Supreme Being, for the universe being an expression of the Shakti, and Shakti being an aspect of the Supreme Being, the world with all its imperfections would also have been an aspect of the Supreme Being. So in order to preserve the nature of the Supreme Being from being polluted - which is their main concern - they again shift their ground and regard Shakti as a principle eternally distinct from the Supreme Being. In this way their attempts to preserve the reality of the world without thereby detracting from the transcendence and perfection of the Supreme Being have always proved to be a fiasco, for if the world is real, it must have a place in the Ultimate Reality, but the very transcendent nature of the Ultimate Reality denies any such place to it. A God who is a creator ceases to be merely transcendent.

From the above it is clear that the logical position of the Pancharatra thinkers is non-dualistic, but as they cannot rest content with it, they try to maintain the reality of the world as well, inspite of the fact that their premises do not permit them to do so. Consequently we find in their teachings a juxtaposition between non-dualism and Realism and their views oscillate between these two tendencies. The failure on their part to be consistent results in serious ambiguities, an instance of which can be seen in how the same passages which are used by Dr. Schrader to prove that 'Illusionism is altogether absent in them'[11], are utilised by P. T. S. Aiyangar to establish Advaitism as the view towards which the Samhitas incline'[12]. Consistency in thinking requires that we must either deny reality to the creation and the creative manifold, or must accept the creative manifold to be an expression of the Absolute. But it is difficult to accept a creative manifold along with an unchanging Absolute. The Pancharatra thinkers try to accept both the positions and with the help of the Principle of Shakti they unsuccessfully try to reconcile the two but at no moment can they find escape either in Realism or in Transcendentalism. They bring in the principle of Shakti to bridge the gulf between the Supreme Being and the world but when it is realised that the two cannot be regarded as really distinct for that would affect Its divine nature, they immediately rush to identify the two.[6] Consequently they find themselves facing an unhappy dilemma. Either they must regard Shakti as identical with the Supreme Being and thus sacrifice Its unchanging and transcendent nature, or they must declare that the two are distinct and thus abandon the concept of divine supremacy. As neither of the positions is comfortable, they leave the problem unsolved and find an escape in a 'half-way house'.

References :

1. Narada Pancharatra II. 2. 100, Jayakhya IV. 85, Parama I. 80
2. 340. 22, 24, 32, 42 ; 348. 12, 13 etc.
3. 350 16, 27
4. 341 89
5. 340. 66
6. 348. 45
7. 340. 33-41

8. Ahirbudhnya V. 4.ff., XIV 7-8, Parama Prakasha I.I.53 etc.
9. Lakshmi Tantra VI 23-25.
10. See Schrader 'An introduction to the Pancharatra and Abirbudhnya Samhita' and Das Gupta - History of Indian Philosophy Vol. III.
11. Loc. cit P. 32-3
12. Outline of Indian philosophy pp 184-5.

CHAPTER IV

THE NATURE AND THE DESTINY OF THE INDIVIDUAL SELF

Introduction

Metaphysics is the consideration of what is involved in the facts of experience. One of the most striking phenomena revealed in experience is the existence of finite spiritual entities, named as individual selves. Though we know what the self is, we do not know what its nature and destiny are. These have occasioned much speculation and sometimes scepticism. We are led to such questions as, what is the status of the individual selves within the system of the universe? Are they real individuals existing in their own right, or are they real modes of a single absolute Reality or are they mere vanishing appearances of the Absolute, who is the only Real?

The Pancharatra thinkers, because of their predominant religious interest, concentrate much of their thought on the theological considerations like the nature of Brahman, emanation of the world out of Brahman, or the means of attaining release from bondage. They are very little interested in psychological speculations irrelevant to their theological purposes. Hence they seldom take into consideration the problem of the nature of the individual self. They however consider in detail, though not with much clarity and consistency, the relation of the individual self to the supreme self.

The Narayaniya account of the individual self

The Narayaniya regards the individual self as dependent on the Supreme being. At times the self-hood of the individual as distinct from the Supreme Being does not gain recognition, but sometimes the individuality of the finite self is clearly discerned. Of the three states of existence in which the individual self can be conceived to exist, the Narayaniya says nothing about its existence prior to the embodied state. Even about the embodied state there are very few and scattered references. But the state of release is described in full detail.

In the embodied state the individual self is pervaded by the Supreme Being, as its Inner Self. The immanence of the Supreme Being in the individual self is so much emphasised that at times It seems to usurp the place of the individual self. Nevertheless the two are not identified with each other. The individual self is regarded as suffering from imperfections, but the Supreme Being is not thought to be affected by them. With regard to the imperfections and evils It is merely a spectator, but Its relation to the embodied self is that of active love and interest.[1] One thing needs to be made clear here that the Supreme Being in Its transcendental aspect is not related to the embodied self. It is only Vasudeva, the personal aspect of the Supreme Being, who is related to the embodied Self and who appears in repeated incarnations for the good of the individual self.

The topic of the relation of the individual self to the Supreme Being in the state of release is not dealt with in a manner free from ambiguity. At times the oneness of the individual self and the Supreme Being is so much emphasised that this explicitly amounts to 'cessation of existence'.[2] Under the Advaitic influence the Narayaniya declares, 'the cessation of separate conscious existence by identification with the Supreme Being is the highest condition for a living being to attain'.[3] To enter into the Supreme Being and to be merged in It, is more to be desired than all other ends. The released ones are said to enter the Supreme Being.[4]

While the Narayaniya thus at times tends to blur all distinctions between the Supreme Being and the individual self, at other times, this extreme view seems to be somewhat modified. For example, while describing the process through which the individual self becomes liberated we are told that the individual self gradually loses all its material qualities till it is completely free from everything and finally enters the Supreme Being.[5] It gives a pictorial description of the entering of the individual self into the Supreme Being.[6] The assumption underlying such description seems to be that though the individual self becomes practically identical with the Supreme Being making it impossible for us to distinguish it from the Supreme Being, it is not entirely identical with It. This is confirmed by the earlier part of the chapter 363 which reads, 'the divine Surya is the refuge of innumerable wonders.

Innumerable munis crowned with ascetic success, together with all the deities, reside in the rays of the Surya, like birds perching on the branches of a tree.'[7] Along with this the description of the emancipated beings found in the Shveta-dvipa suggests that though the individual self, released from the world, is very similar to the Deity in its effulgence, glory and freedom from material qualities it is quite distinct from the Deity and is engaged in devout worship and adoration of the Deity.[8]

From the presence of the above two sharply distinct tendencies we may get at this conclusion that the idea of the final entrance into the Supreme Being and of being merged in It was not clear before the emergence of the Pancharatra thinkers of the Narayaniya. It is also possible that on this problem which is said to relate to a 'deep mystery' the Pancharatra school was divided into two camps, one leaning towards the advaitic and the other towards the non-advaitic view. Or it may be that the two different kinds of the individual selves, namely the released and the ever-free, have two different sorts of relations to the Supreme Being. The ever-free selves continue in existence and do not aspire for the absorption into the Supreme Being or for the 'annihilation of conscious existence' which is the highest end.[9] Instead of the path of emancipation they have adopted the path of pravrtti.[10] It is thought that these ever-free beings are created by the Deity for certain functions that they have to perform. But the released selves attain the highest end of cessation of the conscious existence. From the non-dualistic ontological position of the Pancharatra school it follows that ultimately all the individual selves are to be reabsorbed into the Supreme Being which is the only reality. The state in which the ever-free selves exist is phenomenal only and is on a lower plane.

The Samhita account of the individual self

In consonance with the Advaitic tendency of the school the Pancharatra Samhitas describe the nature and destiny of the individual self in an Advaitic manner. When the Samhita-thinkers think in terms of concepts borrowed from the Advaita the self-hood of the individual self as distinct from the Supreme Being does not get recognition, but when they are guided by religious feelings, they appear to recognise the individual self as distinct from the Supreme Being. They very often do so while considering the individual self in its embodied state. This becomes clear when we consider the relation of the Supreme Being to the individul self in its three states of existence, viz., before the embodied state, in the embodied state and after the embodied state.

The individual self before the embodied state

Regarding the existence of the individual self before the embodied state the Samhitas maintain that the Supreme Being Itself appears as the numerous finite selves and exists in their bodies in their form, there being no other finite selves in the body beyond

It. The Narada Pancharatra declares, therefore, Para Brahma is the eternal Being. It alone is the eternal Individual Self. It is the Inner Self of all and is present in every self.[12] The same is reiterated in a more forceful manner in the Vishnu Samhita which says that the seers of truth declare that one and the same self, is existing in the many. He alone is the individual self, the Inner self and the Supreme Self'.[13] The Padma Samhita declares, 'The atman of the Para and the Kshetrajna are one. The limitation of the Kshetrajna is known to be due to the difference of bodies, as one image is differentiated into many in many images.' 'As the akasha in a pot moves when the pot is moved, truly there is no difference between the Para and the Jiva'.[14] The same theory we find in the Parama Samhita and in the Jayakhya Samhita.[15] This clearly suggests that the Pancharatra thinkers believed in the Advaitic doctrine of avaccheda-vada. The Narada Pancharatra explicitly supports the other Advaitic doctrine of 'bimbapratibimbavada' It declares that the individual self is nothing but a reflection of the Supreme Being. It gives the illustration of the reflection of the sun in the water and in the mirror.[16] The illustration of the reflection of the sun in the mirror is found in the the Vishnu Samhita as well.[17]

Though the Samhitas thus tend to blur all distinctions between the Supreme Being and the individual self, at some places quite inconsistently they insist on the difference between the two. In the

Vishnu Tilaka this distinction is expressed in clear terms as, 'there is a triad here : Brahman, Jiva and Jagat ; Brahman is a mass of light, Jàgat a mass of elements and Jiva a mass of knowledge.'[18]

In spite of the presence of such passages in which the Advaitic tendency is set aside, the predominating tendency of the Samhitas is Advaitic. The relation of the individual self to the Supreme Being is described in a langnage so thoroughly Advaitic that the influence of that philosophy is indeed beyond question. Certainly there are some non-advaitic passages but one cannot explain away this predominating Advaitic tendency as 'an intrusion into the Pancharatra of certain foreign elements.'

The individual self in the embodied state

With regard to the embodied state of the individual self the Samhitas maintain that it is pervaded by the Supreme Being as its soul or principle of consciousness. 'The Supreme Being is the atma of all beings, their ego called Hari.'[19] So much is the Supreme Being regarded as the soul of the individual self that at times It seems to usurp its place. For example the Parama Samhita writes, '...... in the same way the Supreme Purusha though one Himself, assumes in this world of ours different forms according to the ingredient qualities, and thus becomes the bound ones and the released.'[20]

Though the Supreme Being is thus identified with the individual self, yet a distinction is maintained between the two. The two are said to differ with regard to their form, power and knowledge.

The individual self, which originally being one with the Supreme Being, is omnipresent, omnipotent and omniscient, becomes atomic, impotent and ignorant due to the three taints or fetters of Karma.[21] It is only because of this difference that the individual self in its embodied form is derived from the Supreme Being after a long series of emanations during wnich it gradually acquires the properties of matter, and thus becomes further removed from the nature of the Supreme Being.

The individual self in the state of release

In consonance with the Advaitic tendency of the school the state of emancipation of the individual self is described in a language so thoroughly Advaitic using the Advaitic terms 'Samyapatti', 'ekibhavati' etc. that here also an influence from that quarter is quite apparent. The state of emancipation is described as 'becoming Brahman', 'entering into Brahman', 'merging with Brahman' and the like.[22] Further, emancipation is described as the true knowledge of Brahman, which can be attained only through identity -consciousness.[23] The Parama Samhita explicitly maintains that in the release there is complete coalescence of the individual self with Brahman. It declares, 'They (individual selves), become myself alone, there is no difference whatsoever between the two.'[24] In the Padma Tantra it is asked, 'what is the difference, Highest spirit, between Thee and the liberated soul?' and the reply is, they (the liberated souls) become I, there is no difference whatever. As I live just so lives the liberated soul.'[25] Here it may be noted that this verse does not suggest that the liberated souls continue to exist along with Brahman, as Dr. Schrader has interpreted it.[26] What it suggests is that the individual souls live only in so far as the Supreme Being lives, that is, only in Its living and not with any distinct existence of their own. The Jayakhya Samhita illustrates the state of release in the following fashion, 'just as logs of wood enter into the fire and are lost in it, and just as rivers lose themselves in the ocean, so do the Yogins enter into the essence of Brahman.'[27] The Ahirbudhnya Samhita (Chapter XXXI. 7ff) uses the attributes like sarvaga, sarvabhrta etc. for the individual self, which can be applied only if it is identical with the Supreme Being.

But sometimes the Samhitas do not adhere to this Advaitic tendency and maintain the difference between the Supreme Being and the released soul. The Padma Samhita, for example, mentions three types of release, viz. of difference, of identity and of a mixed nature. But it is the release of identity which is regarded as the highest.[28] The Ahirbudhnya Samhita (VI. I. ff.) teaches that the mode of life in the liberated state depends upon the devotional inclination of the individual self in the embodied state.

The distinction between the Supreme Being and the individual soul is further apparent from the fact that most of the Samhitas admit the existence of the ever-free souls which are described as atomic or of the size of a mote. They are referred to as coadjutors of the Lord. This can, however, be explained by stating that this distinction is not between the Supreme Being and the ever-free souls, but only between the immanent Deity and the ever-free souls. The ever-free Souls have place in the immanent reality only and not in the transcendent Absolute.

From the above it is quite clear that the predominating note of the Pancharatra school with regard to the nature and destiny of the individual soul is mainly Advaitic, though non-Advaitic elements also find their appearance there. This of course is not to deny the possibility of there being minor sects of the Pancharatra which did not believe in Advaitism. But merely on the basis of this, one should not explain away the Advaitic passages, which occur so frequently, as 'merely a formal borrowing' from the Advaita, or as 'intrusions of foreign elements'. Dr. Schrader, who subscribes to this view, starts with the presumption that 'the general trend of the Pancharatra is clearly non-Advaitic'. On the basis of this presumption he maintains that the view that 'the soul ever actually becomes one with the Lord is excluded by the premises of the system'.[29] But one can also establish on the contrary that the Advaitism is the view towards which the Samhitas incline.[30] Further, the Advaitic tendency need not be regarded as foreign intrusion because the idea of attaining unity with, and losing identity in, the Deity, is not alien to the fervent mystic temperament of the followers of this cult.

The Advaitic nature of the Pancharatra thought is further evident from the various accounts of the

Pancharatra given in other works. Shankara, for example, in the Uttpatyasambavadadhikarana of his Brahma Sutra Bhashya asserts that the Pancharatra school regards the Individual self as an emanation from the Supreme Being destined to be re-absorbed in It, but constituting during the intermediate period a being at once real and distinct from the Supreme Being. The same is reiterated by Bhamatikara (I.4.21) who quotes Parama Samhita (XII.65) which explicitly states that the difference between the individual self and the Supreme Being persists during the embodied state only, but when release is obtained there remains no difference, since that which causes difference ceases to exist.[31] Kshemaraja in the Pratyabhijnahridaya describes the Pancharatra school as teaching the identity of God and nature (i. e. Pantheism) and regarding the individual self as a fulguration arising out of God.[32] P.T.S. Aiengar writes, 'The relation between the individual soul ....and the Paramatma, is much nearer the advaitic position than would be palatable to the modern vishishtadvaitins.'[33]

Appraisal

From the foregoing consideration it is quite evident that the Pancharatra school has come very much under the Advaitic influence, so much so that it would not be proper to maintain that with regard to the nature and destiny of the individual self the stand taken by the Pancharatra thinkers is realistic. Though the Pancharatra school is thus very much wedded to Advaitism, its instinctive theism does not permit it to be confined to Advaitism, and the result is that both the Advaitic and non-Advaitic tendencies simultaneously appear at certain places. The Pancharatra thinkers have made no efforts to synthesise these two. However, the predominating tendency of the school is Advaitic the non-advaitic tendency appearing to be a later inclusion. The Pancharatra school, like other systems of Indian thought, is not a product of one age or one generation, but has a long history whose major part is unknown to us. It may be that the original Pancharatra school was thoroughly Advaitic and later on made a compromise with non-advaitic tendencies. Though the Pancharatra school may have reached a compromise with non-advaitic (mainly Vishishtadvaitic) tendencies, it did not give up its original Advaitic position. Because of the presence of some non-advaitic elements in the Pancharatra, it would be wrong to conclude that the positions of the Pancharatra school and the Vishishtadvaitic school are identical. A comparison of the Pancharatra position with the position of Ramanuja, the leading Vishishtadvaitin, will show this to be true.

The individual self in the Pancharatra school, as we have seen, is not an entity different from the Supreme Being. It is regarded as a part of Lakshmi, which, like the Maya of the Advaita, is a principle of differentiation, and which ontologically has no independent status. Lakshmi here is more an assumption to explain the manifoldness than an existence. Apparently it is said to be different from the Supreme Being but ultimately it is nothing but Brahman Itself. Just as in the Advaita the individual self is Brahman only, being conditioned by Maya, so also in the Pancharatra school the individual self is regarded to be a fulguration of Brahman caused by Lakshmi. It has, therefore, no ontological status of its own. As to how it comes out as a fulguration of Brahman is explained with the help of the three well-known Advaitic similes, viz., pot in air, pot in water and one figure being reflected in many mirrors. All this is in flagrant opposition to the position of Ramanuja. His uncompromising realism, his anxiety to refute Mayavada, and his vigorous fight for preserving the reality, individuality and inalienability of the individual self are altogether absent in the Pancharatra school.

The Pancharatra school, unlike Ramanuja, further maintains that the individual self has no permanent existence. Since it is a fulguration of Brahman, it is destined to be reabsorbed in It. This view that the individual self is not an imperishable entity, is a logical consequence of the pure monism of the Pancharatra thinkers to whom the Supreme Being is the only reality. The Supreme Being of the Pancharatra thinkers is an Impersonal Absolute for whom the individuals count for little. The natural consequence is that the thought that Brahman is the Supreme Real, easily led them to think that It is the only Real. It is true that to some of them the individual self is too sensibly real to be dismissed as unreal. Under the assumption of common-sense and perhaps under the influence of Vishishtadvaita they did not carry their Advaitic views to their logical consequences. Nevertheless the dominant thought of the Pancharatra school is that the finite self is identical with the Supreme Self. It is only with this presumption that in the first chapter of the Ahirbudhnya Samhita in Narada's hymn (as also in XXXV. 81-91) Ahirbudhnya, a bound soul, is praised as the Absolute One (Svatantra), ever-satisfied One (Nityatripta), Creator and Destroyer of the universe etc.

Further, the relation of the individual self, in the state of release, to Brahman is described in a thoroughly Advaitic language with a manifest tendency to regard the two as identical. The state of release is very often denoted by words like ekibhavati, abhinnam brahmanisthitam, vishet param, brahma-bhavapatti, apunarbhavata etc. Moreover we also come across the Advaitic concepts of Krama mukti and Jivana mukti.

The Pancharatra school is Advaitic not only in its description of the state of release, but also in its account of the means of emancipation. It declares that the knowledge of identity with Brahman leads one to liberation from bondage and the result is coalescence with Brahman.[34] Since the individual self is regarded as nothing else but Brahman, what is necessary for release is to realise this fact. That is why identity-consciousness is regarded as the means of emancipation. Besides knowledge, yogic discipline is also emphasised as a means of emancipation. This is because the yogic discipline is very helpful in annihilating the sense of individuality.

Another Advaitic feature of the Pancharatra philosophy which differentiates it from the Vishishtadvaita of Ramanuja is that it holds that the individual self is essentially all-pervasive and only in the state of bondage it is reduced to atomic size by the Nigraha power of the Lord. The individual self in the state of yoga is described as Sarvaga, Sarvabhuta etc. which indicate its all-pervasiveness. Ramanuja, on the other hand, urges that the individual self in all its states is atomic only. He does so in order to safeguard the reality and inalienable individuality of the individual self. He enters on a severe controversy against Advaitism in which the individual self is regarded as all-pervasive.

The unique contribution of Ramanuja to the Vedanta philosophy is his view that the individual self is an eternal part or body or attribute of Brahman. This doctrine is altogether absent in the Pancharatra school. As a matter of fact no attempt is made in the Pancharatra school to put forth a systematic theory about the relation of the individual self to Brahman.

Lastly, Ramanuja recognises the multiplicitv of the individual self as an ontological fact, but in the Pancharatra school, this multiplicity comes into existence from the Kutastha Purusha long after the process of creation at the lower secondary stage. Not only that, the distinction of the individual selves from Brahman and their plurality seem to be purely verbal in the Pancharatra, as is evident from the nature of release which is said to consist in the union with Brahman.

It may, therefore, be concluded that the basic position of the Pancharatra school with regard to the nature and destiny of the individual self is Advaitic. Considered critically we find that the Pancharatra doctrine of the nature and destiny of the individual self does not seem to be convincing. Whatever be the nature of the practical Pancharatra, its theoretical position appears to be too sweeping to retain individual existence and initiative. Such a theory which regards obliteration of the self as the ultimate end of life, provides no satisfactory status for the individual selves who shrink into the position of nothing, rather than being active cooperators with God in the spiritual enterprise. Further, it is quite perplexing and unintelligible as to why Brahman to which there is nothing unaccomplished, should energise Shakti, Its so-called creative counterpart, to produce a plurality of finite existences which are destined to be reabsorbed. With the help of the principle of Shakti the Pancharatra thinkers could explain as to how the unity breaks up into multiplicity, but they failed to explain the 'why' of this problem. If the multiplicity is nothing but phenomena destined to be destroyed, there is no good reason for spending in vain a stupendous amount of energy for its creation and maintenance. Further under this view all human values would become fragmentary experiences to be transcended. But if these values have no place in the ultimate Reality, why should human beings strive hard to attain and retain them? In a true system of philosophy instead of being annulled these values should be accepted as one of the available clues to the Ultimate Reality.

It is of course a sound principle that the individual can find its meaning within the context of the Absolute. It is the very of aim of all true philosophy and religion to bring the individual into tune with the infinite. But this does not mean depriving the individual of its uniqueness and permanent value. The universal, on the contrary, respects the individual life and lavishes its energy for the attainment of its fulness and abundance. There is indeed a force working for an even richer and more inclusive unity but there is also a tendency working for more and more individuation. The highest kind of unity is not a static unity of a solitary self-centered Absolute, but a dynamic unity of a society of souls realising their highest perfection in love and in mutually enriching fellowship. This is possible where each individual has a unique life of its own and respects the individuality of others, yet where each, not loses, but finds itself in others. God Himself is love and needs such a society (Madbhaktah me priyah). Such is the teaching of the Gita which declares the consummation of the divine purpose to be the establishment of such a divine society. God also is not something away from the earth in a heaven, but exists in us all in the form of an ideal tendency. The relation between God and the individual self should not be stated in terms of the relation of one finite being to another. To regard God as merely an individual caring for praises and offerings of the finite is to fall far short of a highest insight alike of religion and philosophy. God should not be treated as one of the members of the Divine Society, rather He Himself is the Divine Society. When the Upanishads speak of 'entering into Brahman' they perhaps suggest that the individuals become members of this Divine Society. This is the vision which the Vedic and the Upanishadic seers had when they declared, 'Tadvishnoh paramam padam sada pashyanti surayah'. (Ṛigveda 1.22.20., Katha 1.3.9.)

References and footnotes

1. Narayaniya 340.74-102
2. Ibid 341.8,11
3. Ibid 343.79
4. Ibid 335.42-43
5. Ibid 345.13-18
6. Ibid 363.16-18

7. Ibid 363.2-3
8. Ibid 337.32,33,35
9. Ibid 341.11
10. Ibid 341.12
11. Ibid .341.54-76
12. जीवस्तु प्रतिबिम्बश्च भोक्ता सुखदुःखयोः ।
प्रलीयते पुनस्तत्र प्रतिबिम्बो यथारवेः ।।
यथैव शातकुम्भेषु निर्मलेषु जलेषु च ।
प्रत्येकं प्रतिबिम्बश्च दृश्य एव हि जीविनाम् ।।
पुनः प्रलीयते सूर्ये गतेषु च घटेषु च ।
एवं चन्द्रस्य बोद्धव्यं दर्पणे जीवने यथा ।।
तस्मान्नित्यं परं ब्रह्म स जीवो नित्य एव सः ।
सर्वान्तरात्मा भगवान् प्रत्यक्षं प्रतिजीविषु ।।
Narada Pancharatra II.1.29-34
13. Supra-F.N. 70, of Chapter II
14. I. 4.14-15
15. Supra-F.N. 62,63 and 64 of Chapter II
16. Above F.N. 12
17. Above F. N. 13
18. II. 34-35
19. Lakshmi Tantra II-12
20. Supra F.N. 64, of Chapter II
21. (अ) ज्ञानक्रियासमायोगात् सर्ववित् सर्वकृत्सदा ।
अनणु वृचाप्यसंकोचान्मद्भावायोपपद्यते ।।
Lakshmi Tantra XIII 32.

(आ) आकारस्य तिरोधानादणुत्वं पुंस इष्यते ।
Ahirbudhnya Samhita XIV 18.

22. 'ब्रह्मभावापत्ति', 'भगवत्तामयी मुक्ति'—

Ahirbudhnya Samhita XIV-3 also Vishnu Tilaka I. 33

'वैष्णवं तद्विशेत्पदम्' Ahirbudhnya Samhita XIV. 41

'ब्रह्मसमापत्ति' Jayakhya IV. 52

'ब्रह्मसंयुज्यतेपरम्' Ibid IV. 50

चिद्रूपमात्मतत्त्वं यदभिन्नं ब्रह्मणि स्थितम् । Ibid III. 14

ऐक्यं प्राप्नोति-षा मुक्तिः उक्ता सायुज्य लक्षणा ।

मुक्तिर्वाऽस्त्येकतापत्तिर्जीवात्म'परमात्मनोः ॥

Padma Samhita quoted from Advaita Grantha Kosha Sangraha

23. (अ) ब्रह्माभिन्नात्ततो ज्ञानाद् ब्रह्मसंयुज्यते परम्

Jayakhya IV. 50

(आ) ज्ञानेन तदभिन्नेन........जायते ब्रह्मसंसवित

Ibid IV. 38

See also Supra F.N. 69 and 71, of Chapter II

24. अहमेव भवन्त्येते न भेदस्तत्र कश्चन ।

यथाऽहं विहराम्येव तथा मुक्ताश्च देहिनः ॥

Parama Samhita I. 69

25. I. 4.14-15

26. Introduction to the Pancharatra etc. P. 91

27. सरित्संघाद्यथा तोयं संप्रविष्टं महोदधौ ।

अलक्ष्यश्चोदके भेदः परस्मिन् योगिनां तथा ॥

Jayakhya Samhita IV. 121

यथाऽनेकेन्धनादीनि संप्रविष्टानि पावके ।
अलक्ष्याणि च दग्धानि तद्वत् ब्रह्मण्युपासका: ।।

Ibid IV. 123

यथा हि वह्निना लीढमिन्धनं तन्मयं भवेत् ।
एवं चिता समालीढं चेत्यं चिन्मयतां व्रजेत् ।।

Lakshmi Tantra XIV 7 cf. Padma Tantra I. 6.51-52

28. भेदेन चाप्यभेदेन मिश्रेण च चतुर्मुख ।
त्रिधैव मुक्तिरुदिता भेदे कैंकर्य लक्षणा ।।
अभेदे मुक्तिरत्यन्तमैक्यं स्यात्परजीवयो: ।
आत्मनो भावना चैक्यं सोऽहमित्यैवात्मिका ।।

Padma Samhita - quoted from Advaita Grantha Kosha Sangraha

29. Loc. cit P. 91

30. Aiengar, Outlines of Indian philosophy pp. 184-185

31. आमुक्ते भेद एव स्याज्जीवस्य च परस्य च
मुक्तस्य च न भेदोऽस्ति भेदहेतोरभावत: ।।

Parama Samhita XII. 65 quoted by Bhamati Kara (I. 4.21)

32. परा प्रकृतिर्भगवान्वासुदेव: तद्विस्फुलिंग प्राया एव जीवा: इति ।
Pratyabhijnahridaya P. 17, Srinagar Edition

33. Loc. cit. P. 184

CHAPTER V

MEANS OF EMANCIPATION

Introduction

The individual life in the worldly state is incomplete and points beyond itself. It has a goal to achieve, a purpose to fulfil and an end to realise. All systems of Indian philosophy, except the Charvakas and the allied schools, maintain that the ultimate end of human life is to transcend the mundane life of travail. But they differ widely with regard to the nature of the life attained after this transcendence, and also with regard to the means by which this transcendence can be achieved. Broadly speaking three means of emancipation viz., Karma, Jnana and Bhakti, are recognised; but in some systems all the three are taken collectively whereas in some only one or two are enjoined.

Of this triadic process the Advaita school recognises Jnana alone as the final means of emancipation. This is the logical conclusion of its metaphysical position. According to this school bondage consists in being ignorant of the true nature of the self and therefore it is knowledge alone, a discrimination of the real from the unreal, which can bring about release. It, however, recognises ethical discipline and devotion as accessories to intellectual penetration and discrimination inasmuch as they help us in urging to know the Real and in equipping us for that knowledge.

According to the Mimamsa school performance of actions in accordance with scriptural instructions can bring about release. The Advaita school, on the contrary, declares that Karma is inherently incapable of removing ignorance, for it is life in ignorance. Release is not possible with a perception of difference and Karma is not possible without a perception of it. The Advaita school, therefore, bifurcates scripture into Karmakanda and Jnanakanda, and declares that it is the latter alone which is the means of emancipation. In the Jnanakanda again there are two different parts, viz. Paravidya and Apara vidya, and the former alone leads to release. Thus they alone obtain release whose self is enlightened by Para vidya which consists of identity-consciousness.

This identity-consciousness is possible only to those who are equipped with the four requisites, viz. (i) viveka (ii) vairagya (iii) shama, dama, uparati, titiksha and samadhana, (iv) mumkshutva. To these four requisites the Practice of Shravana, Manana and Nidhidhyasana is further necessary. All these elements involve the yoga process of concentration. The Advaita system thus covers the whole ground of Yoga, but while in the Yoga system emancipation proceeds from understanding the difference between purusha and Prakrti, in the Advaita it comes by the dawn of right knowledge that Brahman alone is the true reality.

In the system of Ramanuja emancipation is not a matter of direct realisation of something which is existent from eternity, though hidden from our view, but it is something which is to be attained through rigorous discipline and proper endeavour. According to him bondage is undoubtedly due to ignorance, but it cannot be negated by mere intellectual enlightenment. It requires a course of sadhana—moral, intellectual and spiritual—and consequent mental make-up on the part of the finite and also an insurge of redemptive grace on the part of the Infinite.

In the Pancharatra school the means of emancipation are two-fold, viz., Yoga and Devotion. The Yoga method is mainly Advaitic but the method of Devotion is not so. The peculiarity of the Pancharatra school is that though its ideal is Advaitic one of the means to realise it, viz. devotion, is non-advaitic. We shall now see the Pancharatra account of the means of emancipation in the Narayaniya as well as in the Samhita.

The Narayaniya account

With regard to the means of emancipation the position of the Narayaniya thinkers is mostly non-advaitic. Though it is maintained that the individual self can attain emancipation by knowledge and Yogic practices, yet it is emphasised that above all there must be an exclusive spirit of loving devotion which is the way beloved to the Deity. It is declared, "without doubt the religion of devotion seems to be superior and is very dear to Narayana. The end that is attained by Brahmanas who attending to due observances study the Vedas with the Upanishads and by those that adopt the religion of asceticism, is inferior to that attained by persons devoted to Hari with their whole souls.[3]

Connected with devotion on the part of the devotee there is redemptive grace on the part of the Deity. 'That person upon whom Narayana looks with compassion succeeds in becoming awakened'.[3] But the grace of God, though entirely dependent on God, is not unconditional. It does not fall upon any undeserving one. It is conditioned by renouncing of the evil qualities and pursuing the good ones.

The Samhita account

Narayaniya account does not seem to be very much different from the position of the Gita. But when we turn to the Samhitas we find that in different Samhitas, or also in the same.Samhita, different ways of achieving emancipation are described. It seems that no one taken in itself is regarded as sufficient, but all are required to be synthetically implemented for this task. All these different ways can be broadly brought under two heads, to wit, Yoga and Devotion. The path of Yoga is Vedic but the path of Devotion, named also as Sattvata Vidhi, is Tantric.[4] Though a distinction is made between the two methods of attaining the highest Reality and though the latter alone is regarded as superior and preferable, yet it is emphasised that a devotee must necessarily be initiated in the Yoga vidhi.[5] It seems that the Yoga method is regarded as a preliminary to the path of Devotion. Dr. Schrader has rightly opined that the Yoga method has entered into the Pancharatra through the impact of the Advaita school.[6]

The Path of Yoga

Yoga in the sense of the ultimate end of life is described in the Samhitas as the joining of the individual and the Supreme Self.[7] The methods of Ashtanga and Shadanga yogas and their application to the path of Devotion are discussed in detail in various Samhitas. Prof. S. N. Das Gupta has explained in detail, these various Processes of Yoga discussed in the Samhitas and interested readers may refer to his treatment of the Pancharatra school in the third volume of his History of Indian philosophy.

The path of Yoga is interpreted differently in the Parama Samhita, which seems to be very much influenced by the Gita. Yoga, as a method, is defined as a peaceful union of the mind with any particular object.[8] When the mind is firmly fixed on the performance of an action it is called Karmayoga. It functions as a destroyer of sins.[9] When the mind is firmly fixed on acquiring knowledge without being anxious about results, it is called Jnanayoga.[10] Karmayoga means the moral discipline of Yama and Niyama, involving Vrata, Upavasa and virtuous course of action without any selfish end.[11] Jnanayoga means Vairagya and Samadhi. By Vairagya is meant the wisdom by which mind stays unflinchingly in the Supreme Being. Karmayoga leads to Jnanayoga and through Jnanayoga one attains union with the Supreme Being. The same is reiterated in the Jayakhya, Ahirbudhnya, Lakshmi Tantra and other Samhitas.[12] This knowledge also named as 'Vedanta jnana' is the same as the identity-consciousness or the attribute-less (nirvishesha) knowledge which is upheld in the Advaita.[13] In a language directly borrowed from the Advaita the Brahma Samhita declares that the cessation of the worldly existence is possible only by the consciousness of the fact that there is no duality and that Brahman is the only reality. It quotes in support the famous scriptural passage, very often taken resort to by the Advaita, viz., Brahmavid-bhavatibrahma.

The Path of Devotion—Prapatti

Along with the path of Yoga the Pancharatra school reçognises another and easier method of achieving emancipation which is named as prapatti. The basic idea underlying this method is that all that is necessary for salvation is to flee to the Deity for refuge. It emphasises an absolute and unconditional surrender to the Deity and leaving the work of salvation to be done by him. It also implies that the Deity grants salvation to the individual self irrespective of the moral considerations.

The Ahirbudhnya Samhita defines it as 'praying thought.' The contents of the thought are, 'I am a receptacle of sins, naught, helpless; do Thou become my refuge.'[15]

The preliminary to the prapatti is described as namanam' (adoration). It means a spontaneous acceptance of the Deity as the master. Its core is the feeling of dependence. A true adoration or obeisance proceeds naturally without any motive of any kind.[16] The Ahirbudhnya Samhita gives an occult explanation of the word 'namas' as follows, No (na) selfish regard (mamya) for one's self and one's own (svasmin sviye ca)[17].

The process of prapatti consists of six essentials which are as follows : [18]

The first is a firm resolve of the devotee to dedicate himself to God in the spirit of love and subservience.

The second is abstinence from all kinds of disservice to God. The commands of God should on no account be disobeyed.

The third is an unflinching faith in the providence and goodness of God. The idea that God is all-merciful and all-powerful and hence would certainly protect us produces the quality of faith in God's protective power.

The fourth is the spiritual yearning of the soul to take refuge in the Divine.

The fifth is complete self-surrender to God and resignation of the sense of 'I'.

The sixth and the last is feeling of lowliness.

Prapatti, thus, is a prayer for God's help in association with the conviction of one's being full of sin and guilt, and a sense of being totally doomed without the protecting grace of God. Prapatti depends not on one's mere desire. The only requisite of it is a change of heart, a feeling of contrition, and absolute confidence in the saving grace of God. It is not merely a self-sacrifice of the individual for the Supreme, but also the melting of the Divine heart in response to the self-effacement of the prapanna. The individual is required to make no efforts other than to keep himself in the prayerful spirit ; all the rest is done by God. Prapatti, thus, is upaya-jnana and not upaya. It is like a boat on which the passenger merely sits while it is the business of the boatman to do the rest.

The Pancharatra doctrine of prapatti has been accepted and practised by the Shrivaishnava followers of Ramanuja. They find its basis in the Upanishads (cf. Shve. VI. 18, Katha I. 22. etc.), Ramayana (Yuddha kanda XVIII.3.31) etc. They regard the Gita as the manual of the religion of prapatti. On the basis of the nature of prapatti they are divided into two camps, viz., the Vadagalai or the Northern school and the Tengalai or the Southern school. The former emphasises human initiative and effort as an essential requisite condition of getting the grace of God. The grace of God is one among the several means, and should be resorted to only by those who find it difficult to follow other ways of salvation. The latter school, on the other hand, regards prapatti not as a yoga or human endeavour, but as a work completely to be done by God only. It further holds that prapatti is the only way of salvation and it is assisted by no other means. The characteristic diffierence between the two schools is indicated by their nicknames. The northern is called the 'Monkey school' (Markata Nyaya) because it teaches that the soul must co-operate with the Deity in salvation, as the young monkey clings to its mother who carries it to safety; while the Southern school is called the 'Cat school' (Marjara Nyaya) because it teaches that the soul needs nothing for salvation beyond passively submitting to the Deity, as the kitten remains passive while its mother carries it about in its mouth. Both the schools try to read their respective views in the works of Ramanuia, but there is no basis ror their doing so.[19]

Grace of God as the final means of emancipation

The theistic importance of the Pancharatra school lies in its idea of the grace of God. For the sake of His sincere devotees God is said to assume graciously five-fold forms so as to be easily accessible to them. Out of love the Deity actively concerns Himself in seeking to free His worshippers from the samsara. This work is allotted to the Sudarshana portion of Lakshmi, the Supreme Being being too transcendental to be engaged in such matters. In addition to the three well-known powers of creation, preservation and destruction, Lakshmi, or for that matter the Lord, has two more powers called Nigraha and Anugraha, by means of which she prepares and predetermines the soul for bondage and liberation respectively.[20] The bondage, though it has no beginning may have an end by the breaking in of the power of the divine grace, which resembles a 'shower of compassion' coming down upon him who has been 'beheld' by God, (Vishnu samikshita. cf. Katha. 1.2.23. 'yamevaisha vrnute tena labhyate'). The grace of God may break in at any time, the result of which is the annihilation of all past karmas. This grace further causes the soul to discern its goal, turns it to scriptures and teachers, makes it to strive after the goal by means of the recognised system (Samkhya, Yoga etc.), and finally enables it to enter into Brahman. In this way it is the Grace of God which is the final instrument to attain salvation.[21]

Initiation Through Teacher as a Prerequisite for Grace

Although the Deity thus works for salvation, the individual also has his part to play. The Lord Vishnu is the object of human approach, but He can be approached only through the scriptures and the scriptures can be taught only by a teacher. When through the grace of God one begins to have discriminative knowledge, there dawns spiritual inquiry within an individual and he approaches the true preceptor. The teacher, therefore, is the first and primary means to the attainment of the Ultimate Reality through the instruction of the scriptures.

Before a teacher instructs a disciple, he is required to undergo initiation (diksha). The initiation ceremony in the Pancharatra cult has a very important place. There can be no emancipation of an uninitiated. The main idea underlying initiation is the purification of the individual. The Parama Samhita says that no worship should be performed without the teacher's permission. One desirous of having initiation should fall prostrate at the teacher's feet saying, 'I am now seeking refuge with you, and place my body and wealth at your disposal.' The process of initiation consists of five acts, to wit, (a) the individual should bear on his shoulder the symbol of the Deity (tapa), (b) he should put special marks on his forehead (pundra), (c) he should receive a devotional name (nama), (d) he should learn and recite mantras and (e) he should procure an image of the Deity (yaga).[22]

Worship of Idol as Another Prerequisite

In order that emancipation may be obtained besides the instructions of the scriptures through the preceptor, worship is also necessary. No one can realise the Supreme Spirit without a concrete idea of the same, and hence it is necessary that He should be worshipped in the form of images.[23] The Parama Samhita emphatically directs the aspirant for release to worship God only through idols. 'He is to be worshipped only in the visible form. Except in such a form worship ought not to be conducted.' The worship or prayer offered to His image is as good as worship etc. offered to Him directly. The only thing to be taken care of is that the worship should be conducted strictly in the manner prescribed in the ordinances of the Pancharatra.[24]

The worship should always be conducted through mantras, because the mantras are the part and parcel of God. The letters of the alphabet originate from Him, and their combination makes mantras. And because the mantras come out of Him, it is reasonable that His worship should be performed through the agency of the mantras.[25]

In the Sattvata Samhita four kinds of worship are described. These four are enjoined on the devotees of different mental make-up, caste, liking, etc. They are as follows :[26]

(i) The yogins familiar with the eight-fold yoga, satisfied with the worship of the heart are authorised for the worship of the one dwelling in the heart. This worship connected with the diagram of sounds (varnacakra), the six attributes of God etc. is described in detail in the Ahirbudhnya Samhita.

(ii) On the other hand, the brahmanas fond of mixed worship and extolling the Vedas are authorised for the worship, with mantras of the four Vyuhas. They should not worship the Lord in any other way.

(iii) Again, those of the three other castes viz., the kshatriyas etc. who have sincerely taken refuge with the Lord, should also, but not with mantras, perform several rites connected with the worship of the four Vyuhas. The Ahirbudhnya Samhita (chap. XXXVI) teaches that the Sudarshana Yantra consists of form and mantra aspects. The form aspect conists of figures of the Sudarshana Purusha surrounded by the twelve sub-vyuhas, etc. The brahmanas alone can meditate on the mantra aspect. The others are recommended to worship through the form aspect only.

(iv) But for the worship of the mantra diagram relating to thirty nine Vibhavas and for the ceremonies connected with these none are authorised but the truly seeing ones, who have completely cast off the idea of mine, are satisfied with doing their duty and wholly devoted in deed, speech and mind, to the Highest Lord.

This fourth class consists of those brahmanas, among the Pancharatrins, who have abandoned mixed, that is, Vedic worship, and who prefer the path of devotion to that of yoga.

But it is also emphasized that they alone are authorised to do either of these four forms of worship who have embraced the Sattvata religion and who have been dulv initiated with the mantras prescribed.

Shankaracharya in his notice of the Pancharatra school refers to five methods of worshipping the

Supreme Lord which are as follows : (i) Abhigamana, (ii) Upadana, (iii) Ijya, (iv) Svadhyaya and (v) Yoga. They are named as panchakala krityas in the Shri-Vaishnava ethics.[37] It should be noted that the Pancharatra is not only a school of thought but also a body of people practising a mode of worship in conformity thereto. It emphasises the worship of arca or idol, which is one of the five-fold manifestations of the Deity. The major portion of the Pancharatra literature consists of rituals concerning worship, iconography, temple architecture, installing of images etc.

From the foregoing it is clear that the means of emancipation in the Pancharatra school are two-fold, viz., Yoga and Devotion. The yoga method is mainly Advaitic and has very much come under the influence of yoga school. The path of Devotion, specially its prapatti doctrine, is peculiar to the pancharatra, and may be said to be its unique contribution to the philosophy and religion of India. The peculiarity of the Pancharatra school lies in that though its ideal is Advaitic, one of the means, viz.. prapatti, to realise it, is non-advaitic. The Pancharatra school has accepted the monistic philosophy of the Upanishads, appreciated the value of worship and prayer along with the bhakti school, and like the yoga system laid great emphasis on the discovery and culture of the most important bodily centres and processes connected with the mind.

Ramanuja and the Pancharatra school—

A study in contrast

The Advaitic impact on the Pancharatra concept of the means of emancipation can be made clear by contrasting the Pancharatra position with that of Ramanuja's. The fundamental difference between Ramanuja and the Pancharatra school is that the synthetic approach of Ramanuja, under which he co-ordinates karma, jnana, bhakti and grace of God as the integral constituents of the same course of sadhana, is conspicuously absent in the Pancharatra school. Though these concepts do occur in the Pancharatra Sadhana, the meaning put on them is quite different. Unlike Ramanuja, the Pancharatra school advocates two different lines of sadhana, the relation between which has been left undescribed. It seems that the two are regarded as independent and separate means. The one form of Sadhaṇa consists of jnana and karma, with a basis of yoga. This form is mainly Advaitic in nature. Ramanuja also recognises karma and jnana as the stages in the scheme of sadhana, but they are not given independent value. They are merely preliminaries to bhakti. In the Pancharatra school like the Advaita, karma is helpful to the attainment of jnana and it is jnana alone which is the direct means to release. Further by karma Ramanuja means nishkama karma as taught in the Gita, whereas in the Pancharatra school karma is understood as performance of action with complete concentration. Similarly jnana, in Ramanuja, stands for the true knowledge of individual self as different from the body etc. In the Pancharatra school knowledge is understood, like the Advaita, as identity-consciousness, i.e. the consciousness of oneself being identical with the Absolute. The means of developing such a knowledge are vairagya and samadhi, which are again the means recognised in the Advaita school.

Through the Advaita school the whole process of Pancharatra sadhana has very much come under the influence of yoga system. Here the yoga process has occupied such an important place that an aspirant for release is required to be a yogi. The Pancharatra school not merely borrowed the yoga sadhana but also has made substantial improvement upon it.

The other line of sadhana recognised in the Pancharatra school is that of bhakti, or more properly, prapatti. In Ramanuja jnanayoga must ripen into bhakti yoga and bhakti alone evokes the grace of God which results in release. But in the Pancharatra school jnana, not only does not develop into bhakti but also does not stand in need of the grace of God for the attainment of release.

Further, the whole theory and practice of bhakti in Ramanuja is essentially different from that of the Pancharatra, so much so that psychologically speaking they may be said to be just the opposite. In the Pancharatra school bhakti moves in an indefinite haze of mythology (in the Narayaniya) and occultism (in the Samhitas) with a strange combination of sentimentalism. In Ramanuja, on the contrary, it is set forth not only with a systematic philosophic background, but also with an intellectual seriousness and ethical nobility. In the Pancharatra school bhakti, as a matter of fact, is nothing else but prapatti, a spirit of absolute and unflinching surrender to God, leaving aside all other scriptural duties, technically called avidhigocharatva. But in Ramanuja the concept of prapatti is not only altogether absent, but it is also in flagrant contradiction to his declared teaching. The bhakti of Ramanuja is contemplation of God, but the prapatti of the Pancharatra school is an utter self-surrender to God. The goal of bhakti is realisation of God but the goal of prapatti is servitude to God. It is true that the Pancharatra bhakti does not have that much of exuberance of feeling, erotic element and unintellectual emotionalism as we find in the Alvars, yet it is not completely free from these elements. In Ramanuja, on the contrary, bhakti is essentially qualified by karma and jnana, is very much restrained, and consists of calm meditation and serene contemplation. In Ramanuja it stands for intuitive realisation or immediate presentation but such a sublime concept is far from the ritualistic bhakti of the Pancharatra. In the Pancharatra school bhakti has come to assume a mechanically ritualistic outer form, mere heartless repetition of mantras, but in Ramanuja it is essentially inner spiritual attitude enriched by virtues and disciplined by rigorous effort. The bhakti in Ramanuja is a result of sadhana saptaka whereas in the Pancharatra school it is mere spontaneous and unrestrained exhibition of the feeling of surrender. Lastly, the bhakti of Ramanuja takes full regard of the factors of freedom and initiative of the individual, and moral responsibility of God, but both these factors are sadly neglected in the Pancharatra concept of prapatti.

Both Ramanuja and the Pancharatra school recognise the grace of God. To Ramanuja the grace of God is the culminating result of the triadic process of karma, jnana and bhakti, which involves a training of body, intellect and will. In the Pancharatra school out of the two processes recognised for release, it is only the bhakti marga which stands in need of the grace of God, and not the jnana marga. In the bhakti marga, too, the grace of God, unlike Ramanuja, is quite unmerited, and is showered irrespective of the conduct and character of the subject. Not only do they differ with regard to the stimulus for grace, but they also differ with regard to the function of grace. In the Pancharatra school the individual has to play no role except that of self-surrender. The Deity requires no efforts on the part of the individual. But in Ramanuja the grace of God merely removes the obstacle in the path of devotion caused by past sins and generates a tendency towards devotion. The rest is to be done by the individual only. In Ramanuja the grace of

God operates in accordance with the law of karma, but in the Pancharatra school even the Karmas can be annulled by the grace.

Another point of difference between Ramanuja and the Pancharatra school is that unlike the former the latter is very much wedded to the worship of idol (arca). Almost half of the Pancharatra literature consists of the elaborate process of worship, recitation of mantras and other related things. The worship of idol may be regarded to be one of the most important characteristics of the Pancharatra school. It is regarded as almost indispensable for a devotee. In order that one may be entitled to perform worship, he is required to undergo initiation through the teacher. All these processes of worship and initiation have come very much under the influence of tantrism. The worship of idol, the ceremony of initiation in the sect and consequent importance of the teacher and the predominance of tantric element are altogether absent in Ramanuja. As a matter of fact Ramanuja does not belong to any particular sect, though his philosophy has very much influenced the Shri-Vaishnava sect.

References and footnotes

1. Narayaniya 349.4-5.
2. Ibid 349.75-76
3. Ibid 349.70
4. The Ahirbudhnya Samhita describes two different ways for the attainment of the ultimate Reality, viz ;

through mantras and through yoga. (chap. XXX. 4-5). It, however, places more emphasis on the former.

The Jayakhya Samhita also describes these two ways and regards the practice of concentration on the mantras as more efficacious.

5. Dr. S. N. Dasgupta (History of Indian philosophy vol. III P. 32) remarks, 'The so-called bhakti school of the Bhagavatas was so much under the influence of the yoga system that a bhakta was required to be a yogin, since bhakti by itself was not regarded as a sufficient means to the attainment of salvation.'

cf. 'तस्मात्सर्वप्रयत्नेन भाक्तो योगी भवेत्सदा'

—Vishnu Samhita Chap. 30.

6. Loc. cit. P. 91. N. 2.

7. संयोगो योग इत्युक्तो जीवात्म परमात्मनोः ।

Ahirbudhnya Samhita XXXI. 15.

8. यत्करोति समाधानं चित्तस्य विषये क्वचित् ।
अनुकूलमसंक्षोभं संयोग इति कीर्त्यंते ॥

Parama Samhita X. 6.

9. यदि कर्माणि बध्नन्ति चित्तं अस्खलितं नरम् ।
कर्मयोगो भवत्येषः सर्वपाप प्रणाशनः ॥ Ibid X. 7.

10. यदि तु ज्ञान एवार्थे चित्तं बध्नाति निर्व्यथः ।
ज्ञानयोगः स विज्ञेयः सर्वसिद्धिकरः शुभः ॥ Ibid X. 8.

11. साधनं तस्य च प्राक्तो धर्मो निरभिसन्धिकः ।

Ahirbudhnya Samhita XIV. 4.

12. (अ) एवं क्रियाख्यात् सत्ताख्यं ज्ञानं प्राप्नोति मानवः ।
ब्रह्मण्यभिन्नं सत्ताख्यात् ज्ञानात् ज्ञानं ततो भवेत् ।

ब्रह्माभिन्नात्ततो ज्ञानाद्ब्रह्म संयुज्यते परम् ॥

Jayakhya Samhita IV. 49. 50

(आ) सम्प्राप्य ज्ञान भूयस्त्वं निर्मलीकृत चेतनः ।
अनाविलमसंक्लेशं वैष्णवं तद्विशेत्पदम् ॥

Ahirbudhnya Samhita XIV. 41

ज्ञानक्रियेति द्विविधं चेष्टितं सर्वदेहिनाम् ।
ज्ञानाधिक्यात् विमुक्तिस्यात् क्रियाधिक्यात्तु संसृतिः ॥

Ibid. I. 67

ज्ञानेन साध्यते मोक्षः क्रिया ज्ञानस्य शोधिनी ।

Ibid. XII. 59.

(इ) ब्रह्मं नारायणं मां यत् ज्ञानेनैवाप्नुयाद्यतिः ।
पन्था नान्योऽस्ति विज्ञानादयनाय विपश्चिताम् ॥

Lakshmi Tantra XV. II.

(ई) ज्ञाने तस्मिन् समुत्पन्ने विशते माममनन्तरम् । Ibid XV. 13.

13. प्राप्त वेदान्त विज्ञानो वैष्णवं श्रयते पदम् ॥

Ahirbudhnya XV. 53
See Supra f.n. 23 of Chapter IV

14. द्वैतं नास्तीति बोधेन मनसो द्वैतनाशनम् ।
एतदन्तो हि संसारः ब्रह्मन्नैव विचारयन् ॥
सगुणोपासनं हि तावत् साधनं निर्गुणस्य तु ।
ब्रह्मविद् भवति ब्रह्म इत्येषा च परा श्रुतिः ॥

quoted from Advaita Grantha Kosha Samgraha

15. Ahirbudhnya Samhita XXX VII. 30-31.,
cf. Lakshmi Tantra XVI. 43-44., XVII 58-61 etc.

16. Ahirbudhnya Samhita LII. 9, 15

17. Ibid, LII. 28 ; cf 'नास्मि न मे नाहम्' of Samkhya Karika. 64

18. Ahirbudhnya Samhita XXXVII. 27-28; cf. Lakshmi Tantra XVII. 66-67

19. See my paper 'Does Ramanuja Advocate Prapatti doctrine?' Philosophical Quarterly, Jan. 1966.

20. Lakshmi Tantra XII. 14; Ahirbudhnya I. 2; XXI. 12 etc.

21. मया जीवा समीक्ष्यन्ते श्रिया दुःखविवर्जिताः ।
सोऽनुग्रह इति प्रोक्तः शक्तिपातापराह्वयः ॥

Lakshmi Tantra XII. 8

The Parama Samhita gives a different interpretation of the concept of grace. It holds that faith, devotion and meditation on God result in good and that good is grace of God.

श्रद्धा भक्ति समाधिश्च मयि प्रणिहिता जनैः ।
शुभमेव विविच्यन्ते तत्प्रसादमवैहि मे ॥ I. 84.

22. Parama Samhita VIII. 66, 72

23. Jayakhya Samhita V. 29-31

24. Parama Samhita III. 5-66.

25. Jayakhya VI. 59, 60.

26. II. 2-12., See Schrader, Loc. cit. P. 150 ff

27. Jayakhya Samhita XXII. 65-75., Padma Samhita, caryapada, XIII. 3.

INDEX

APPENDICES

Does Bādarāyaṇa Favour Pāñcarātra?

In the *tarkapāda* of the second chapter of the *Brahmasūtra*, the last *adhikaraṇa*, viz., *Utpatyasambhavādhikaraṇa*, is very controversial. It consists of four *sūtras* (numbering II.2.39 to 42 according to Rāmānuja, and II.2.42 to 43 according to Saṃkara). The great *ācāryas* who commented upon it are not agreed upon their interpretation. Saṃkara, Bhāskara, Rāmānuja, Vallabha and Śrīkaṇṭha envisage in it a reference to *Pāñcarātra* school, whereas Nimbārka, Madhva, Baladeva and Sriniwāsa hold that it is directed to the Śākta view.

I

The *ācāryas* who give the *śākta* interpretation do not seem to be convincing. They interpret the first *sūtra* as a refutation of the view that *Śakti* alone, independently of the intelligent being, can create the world. The *sūtra* holds that it is impossible to create the world without the help of puruṣa. This *sūtra* is also interpreted differently. The origin of the world is not possible because it is eternal. As the world is not something produced, *Śakti* cannot be its cause.

The form of the above *sūtra* is mere *'utpatyasambhavāt'*; from this it is quite evident that it has been put forth to refute a particular doctrine. In the first *sūtra* of every *adhikaraṇa* of *tarkapāda*, where Bādarāyaṇa initiates the refutation of other systems, he has always used the characteristic words like *anumāna, hṛsva parimandala, samudāya, abhāva, sarvathānupapatti, ekasmin, pati* etc. which are indicative of the particular schools refuted. In the present *sūtra* also which initiates such a discussion, we may expect of him to have used such a technical word of the system he has intended to refute. The wording of the *sūtra* does not shed sufficient light to enable us to say decisively as to which system it refers.

If we interpret this *sūtra* as a refutation of the *Śakti* view, then we will have to interpret it in a general way,—that from a particular element (viz. *Śakti*) there is no creation of the universe, and theretore it cannot be the cause of the universe. But we have no basis to interpret it so. Nor do we have any other indication, because the word Śakti does not occur in the *sūtra*, and the *Sūtrakāra* has not used any word characteristic of the *Śakti* school.

On the other hand, if we take it as the initiation of the refutation of the *Pāñcarātra* view, then from the wording of the *sūtra* we get the indication of the characteristic doctrine of the *pāñcarātra*, viz., '*parama kāraṇāt parabrahmabhūtāt Vāsudevāt Saṃkarṣaṇo nāma jīvo jāyate*', in the same way in which from the *sūtra* II.2.31 (*ekasminnasambhavāt*) we get the indication of the *Anekāntavāda* of Jainism.

The second *sūtra* is interpreted by them as follows: 'If it is said that in producing the world *puruṣa* helps Śakti, the *sutra* answers that no sense-organ is possible on the part of the *puruṣa* prior to the creation, and without a sense-organ it is not possible for the creator to be the helper.'

The preceding *sūtra*, as we have seen, does not refer to the *Śakti* doctrine, and theretore the present *sūtra* also ipso facto does not refer to the same. But if we concede that in the present *sūtra* there is refutation of the *Śakti* view, then the interpretation given by those commentators would not be in contormity with the context and with the *sūtra* itself. The above commentators hold that the first *sūtra* refutes the view that *Śakti* without *puruṣa* cannot create the world. When in the first *sūtra* itself the help of *puruṣa* is negated, it is out of question to say in the next *sūtra* that *puruṣa* being without instrument cannot be a helper to *Śakti*. Moreover, in the preceding *sūtra*—if we regard it as a reference to the *Śakti* doctrine—only this much is said that *Śakti* cannot produce the universe. Why it cannot produce is not mentioned. Nor is there any reference to *puruṣa*. Then from where the reference to *puruṣa* has been taken and the meaning put that the *puruṣa*, having no instruments, cannot help the *Śakti*? From the word '*Kartuḥ*' in the present *sūtra*, we have a reference to that element only which is referred to as *Kartā* in the preceding *sūtra*, and that element is *Śakti* and not *puruṣa*. If in the present *sūtra* '*kartuḥ*' is accepted for *puruṣa* then in the preceding *sūtra* also the same meaning must be accepted. Lastly, in the present *sūtra* '*kartuh*' cannot stand for '*Śakti*' because it is masculine, and because *Sakti* cannot be said to be without instruments.

The third *sūtra* is explained by this school of commentators as follows: 'if you hold that the *Śakti* is possessed of inherent knowledge etc., then there is no objection, because thereby you have come over to our doctrine of Brahman.'

But this interpretation is also quite untenable. If in any doctrine the creator is regarded as possessed of inherent knowledge etc., this does not mean that that doctrine would become *Brahma vāda* and would be acceptable to the *Sūtrakāra,* nor by such simple modification it would become unassailable in the eyes of the *Sūtrakāra.*

The fourth *sūtra* is interpreted by them as a concluding general condemnation of the *Śakti* doctrine. It does not contain any new argument and hence is not very important. Thus it is clear that this adhikaraṇa is not meant to refute the *Śakti* doctrine.

In the group of *ācāryas* giving *pancarātra* interpretation, which seems to be more convincing, there are wide divergences. Śaṃkara, Bhāskara and Vallabha hold that in it the *Pāñcarātra* is refuted just like other doctrines in the rest of the *pāda.* Bhāskara, however, maintains that he differs from the *pāñcarātra* in regard to its doctrine of the individual souls having been produced from Brahman (II. 2-40); but as the *Pāñcarātra* holds that the Supreme Brahman is both the material as well as the instrumental cause of the world, he is in agreement with it. (Śamkara also attacks only some of the doctrines and tenets and agrees with the rest of them). Vallabha follows Śamkara except in II-2-41, where he explains *'tadapratiṣedhāt'* as *'Īśvarāṇām pratiṣedhāt'* i.e., plurality of the lords. Rāmānuja agrees with Śamkara and Vallabha regarding the interpretation of the first two *sūtras,* but differs with regard to the explanation of the last two *sūtras.* According to him the first two *sūtras* contain objections against the doctrine in question, and thus mention the 'prima facie' view; but the last two *sūtras* refute those objections and ultimately establish the *pāñcarātra* doctrine, which is thus the doctrine held by the *sūtrakāra.*

In this group only two commentators—Śaṃkara and Rāmānuja—deserve our special consideration. Śaṃkara commences by remarking that the *Pāñcarātra* deserves acceptance in so far as it holds that God is both the efficient and the material cause of the world. So also when it says that *Vāsudeva* is the highest Reality, whose nature is pure knowledge, and that He dividing Himself in four parts, appears in four forms as *Vāsudeva* (denoting the Highest Self) *Samkarsana* (individual soul) *pradyumna* (mind) and *Aniruddha* (Principle of egoism), there is nothing to object. Nor is it objectionable to hold that by devotion and meditation we reach the Highest Being.

But Śaṃkara takes exception to the doctrine that Saṃkarṣaṇa, i.e., individual soul, springs from Vāsudeva, i.e.,| the Supreme Lord for it is impossible that the individual soul would spring from the Highest Self, which would make the former non-eternal.

Śaṃkara in the second *sūtra* further rejects it on the ground that observation does not show an instrument (mind) springing forth from an agent (individual soul).

In the third *sūtra* also Śaṃkara rejects it. He writes that even if it be said that in consequence of their being endowed with knowledge etc., *Saṃkarṣaṇa* and others are really all lords, free from faults, and without any imperfections, the following objections may be raised: (i) If the four lords have the same attributes do they not constitute one and the same self? (ii) Here the *pāñcarātra* commits the fallacy of uselessly assuming more than one lord, and thereby contradicts its own principle of one Supreme Lord. (iii) Further, it cannot be maintained that from one Higest Being spring four forms possessing equal attributes, because cause requires pre-eminence over effect; but no such difference is admitted by the *Pāñcarātra.* (iv) Lastly, why to limit the forms of *Vāsudeva* to four only? The whole world from Brahman to a blade of grass should be regarded as a manifestation of the Supreme Being.

The last *sūtra,* according to Śaṃkara, holds that the *Pāñcarātra* doctrine cannot be admitted owing to there being many contradictions in the doctrine itself, and owing to its containing many passages contradictory to the Vedas. It sometimes mentions these four as qualities and sometimes as bearers of qualities. Śāndilya the promulgator of the *Pāñcarātra* system, it is said, was dissatisfied with the Vedas because he could not find in them a satisfactory way of supreme excellence and final beatitude. Therefore he took recourse to the *Pāñcarātra.* This, says Śaṃkara, amounts to saying that the *Pāñcarātra* system is superior to the Vedas.

Thus Śaṃkara holds that the author of the *sūtras* is not in favour of *Pāñcarātra,* though some of its tenets are not unacceptable.

Rāmānuja, however, agrees with Śaṃkara regarding the interpretation of the first two *sūtras* that they are meant to refute some of the tenets of *Pāñcarātra,* but he differs in that these *sūtras* constitute only the *pūrvapakṣa,* i.e., the prima facie view. He holds that the first *sūtra* raises a doubt that the *Pañcarātra* may be destitute of authority in so far as it belongs to the same class of *tantras* as those of Kapil and others. Further the *Pāñcarātra* holds that from

Vāsudeva, who is the highest Brahman and the supreme cause, there originates the individual soul called *Saṃkarṣaṇa*. From *Saṃkarṣaṇa* springs the internal organ called *Pradyumna* and from *Pradyumna* comes the principle of egoity called *Aniruddha*. Now this theory implies the origination of the individual soul and this is contrary to the scriptures, because the scriptural texts declare the soul to be without a beginning.

The second *sūtra* also expresses the inadmissibility of the *Pācarātra* view that the internal organ called *Pradyumna* originates from the individual soul called *Saṃkarṣaṇa*. This is quite opposed to Muṇḍaka II-1.3 which declares that the mind also springs from none else but the highest Brahman.

Now Rāmānuja twists the meaning of the last two sūtras. He holds that the word *'vā'* in the third *sūtra* sets aside the view maintained in the two previous *sūtras*. *'Apratiṣeaṇa'* is taken to mean that there is no contradiction to the *Pāñcarātra*. Rāmānuja says that if *Saṃkarṣaṇa* etc. are of the nature of Supreme Brahman, then truly there cannot be any objection to it. As a matter of fact the *Pāñcarātra* teaches not an impossible origination of the soul, but that the highest Brahman called *Vāsudeva*, out of compassion for the devotees voluntarily abides in a four-fold form, so as to render Himself accessible to them. This is also supported by the scripture, 'not born, He is born in many ways.'

Moreover, *Saṃkarṣaṇa* etc., are the beings ruling over the individual souls, internal organs, and the organs of egoity. There can be no objection to their being denoted in this way. This case is analogous to that of Brahman being designated by the terms like ether, breath and the like

In the last *sūtra* Rāmānuja holds that the doctrine of the origination of *Jīva*, which is brought forth as an objection, is distinctly controverted in the books of the *Pāñcarātra* as well, and hence the objection raised against it on this ground is without any basis. Rāmānuja winds up the *adhikaraṇa* with a long discussion on the authoritativeness of the *Pāñcarātra*, putting forth some arguments in its favour. He writes that the alleged charge of condemning the Vedas imputed to Śāndilya is due to a gross misunderstanding of what he has said. Śāndilya's observations are only to eulogise the *Pāñcarātra* and not to condemn the Vedas. He argues that the *Pāñcarātra* is meant to facilitate the understanding of the Vedas which by themselves are difficult of comprehension. This case is at par with Nārada's words in the Chāndogya VII.2.

Rāmānuja argues that the authority of the *Pāñcarātra* cannot be challenged because the Lord Himself has composed it, to enable his devotees to grasp the true meaning of the Vedas.

Lastly, he pleads for the orthodoxy of the *Pāñcarātra* on the basis of the Mahābhārata, saying that the *sūtrakāra* who is also the author of the Mahābhārata, has maintained the orthodoxy of the *Pāñcarātra* in the Mahābhārata, and hence in the *Sūtras* he cannot repudiate their orthodoxy and thereby contradict himself. Here it may be objected that in the Mahābhārata Sāṃkhya etc. are also mentioned as worthy of regard, but in the *sūtras* those same doctrines are refuted. Why should not the same hold good in the case of the *Pāñcarātra?* The reply that Rāmānuja gives is that the Sāṃkhya etc., are of human origin, whereas the *Pāñcarātra* is of divine origin, and hence its authoritativeness.

Let us now see how far Rāmānuja is true in holding that the *sūtrakara* has favoured and not rejected the *Pāñcarātra*. It is quite evident, as all the commentators agree, that the tone of the first two *sūtras* is combative. The difference of opinion is only with regard to the interpretation of the last two *sūtras*. In the second *sūtra*, holds Rāmānuja, the use of the particle '*vā*' is indicative of the change of side in the argument, both in the Pūrva Mīmāṃsā and Vedānta. One can find such instances in the third *pāda* of the third chapter. But with reference to the context, such an inference does not seem to be warranted. It is true that the *Sūtrakāra* while refuting the origination in the preceding *sūtra*, in this *sūtra* has used the word '*vā*' which indicates that here he is not refuting some of the *Pāñcarātra* doctrines. But this does not mean that it is a change of side. It may be that in this *sūtra* he has given an alternative which though true may not be worthy of importance. Or it may be that in the preceding *sūtras* after refuting the origination, in the present *sūtra* he has given an alternative that if by *mana* we mean knowledge which arises from *Jīva*, then this is not to be refuted. In the *Ups*. also various forms of the knowledge are referred as *mana* (Ait. 5.2, Bṛh. 1.5.3.). The word '*vā*' suggests two alternatives. If the first is accepted, then the *Pāñcarātra* is worth condemnation; and if the second is accepted, then it is not to be refuted. In this respect neither the interpretation of Śaṃkara nor that of Rāmānuja seems to be correct.

Further, in the same *sūtra* Rāmānuja interprets the word '*vijñānādi*' as Brahman which seems to be improper, because nowhere the *sūtrakāra* has used this word in this sense. He always uses it in the sense of *mana* or *buddhi* (e.g., 2.3.16). Nor is this word a technical term in the *Pāñcarātra* school. Similarly Vallabha's interpretation, which is also more or less the same, does not seem to be acceptable.

From the interpretation of Rāmānuja it is quite evident that in the last *sūtra* he has twisted the meaning. Here he explains *'vipratiṣedhācca'* as 'and because the origination of the individual soul is contradicted in this *śāstra*', saying thereby that the objection raised in the first *sūtra* is out of question, since the *Pañcarātra* does not hold this view. But this interpretation is not at all happy. Here he not only explains away the question of origination, but also commits the fallacy of inconsistency. This becomes evident by comparing it with the *sūtra*, 2.2.9., where Bādarāyaṇa uses the same phrase to mean that contradictions in the Sāṃkhya system make it unacceptable to the wise. The interpretation of Rāmānuja that in the *Pāñcarātra* Śāstra itself the origination of the *Jīva* is refuted and therefore the *Pāñcarātra* is regarded as valid by the *Sūtrakāra*, would have been correct provided in the *sūtra* itself instead of *'vipratiṣedhācca'* there would be simply *'pratiṣedhācca'*. *Vipratiṣedha* means mutual contradiction and this is accepted by Rāmānuja as well in 2.2.9.

So far as negation of the origination is concerned, it is found in some sections of the *Pāñcarātra*, but there must have been some section which accepted and preached this doctrine, as is testified by Kṣemarāja in the *Pratyabhijña hṛdaya*. Though the alleged doctrine is not present and also not accepted in the modern *Pāñcarātra* school, and hence the above criticism of the *sūtrakāra* is not now applicable to them, yet the fact remains that the interpretation of Śaṃkara and Vallabha is not incorrect. It must be that at the time of *Sūtrakāra* the *Pāñcarātra* was holding this view, and later on in view of the opposition it has altered this doctrine. Moreover, Rāmānuja while defending this doctrine and arguing that the *Pāñcarātra* does not preach this origination, quotes Parama Samhitā (2.19); but in that Samhitā this verse *'Vāsudevāt Saṃkarṣaṇo nāma jīvo jāyate'* does not occur. It seems that by the time of Rāmānuja those *Pāñcarātra* works which held the origination must have been non-prevalent.

The argument of Rāmānuja that the *sūtrakāra* is also the author of the Mahābhārata etc., is entirely baseless and has no proof for its support. Consequently it carries no weight. Secondly, in the Mahābhārata itself (xii. 349.64), the *Pāñcarātra* is distinguished from the Vedas and is regarded as outside the pale of vedic orthodoxy. Lastly, in the Mahābhārata, Sāṃkhya etc., are also praised but they are condemned in the *sūtra*. The defence of Rāmānuja that the Sāṃkhya etc. are condemned because they are of human origin whereas the *Pāñcarātra* is of divine origin seems to be a lame excuse.

As a matter of fact the *tarkapāda* is meant to refute rival theories, as Rāmānuja himself accepts (*parapakṣa pratikṣepo hyasmin pāde kṛyate* 2.2.10). In the whole of this section the *sūtrakāra* is on the offensive, refuting through reasoning only, without recourse to the scriptual texts. In this section he refutes those schools of thought that were regarded by the orthodox section as outside the sphere of the Vedas. The *Pāñcarātra* was also regarded as outside the pale of the Vedas, and therefore we cannot reasonably expect Bādarāyaṇa to have accepted the *Pāñcarātra* view. Had he intended to favour the *Pāñcarātra*, he should not have dealt with it in the *tarkapāda*. The best place to discuss this would have been 2.3.18, where on the authority of the scripture the *sūtrakāra* negates the origination of the soul and propounds its eternity. Moreover, if the *sūtrakāra* wanted to defend the *Pāñcarātra* he could have done so in a far less ambiguous manner.

The argument of Dr. Thibaut that it is not an unnatural procedure to end the polemical *pāda* with the defence of a doctrine which is to be viewed as true, is without any force, since the exposition and the defence of the true doctrine is the object of the whole book and not of one single *adhikaraṇa* of the *tarkapāda*; and what is more important is that we do not come across in the whole work, any characteristic doctrine of the *Pāñcarātra*, nor do we find the terms *Vāsudeva* etc., so peculiar to the *Pāñcarātra*. The fact that this particular doctrine is refuted last of all, can be explained, as Ghate suggests, by the circumstance that it is most allied to the Vedānta doctrine, and Śaṃkara and Bhāskara have admitted this at the very beginning of this *adhikaraṇa*.

Thus the possible conclusion we can arrive at, on the basis of the above examination, is that the interpretation of Rāmānuja is far-stretched, and though Śaṃkara's interpretation is not fully correct, yet it seems to be nearer to the truth.

Why Pāñcarātra was Condemned as Non-Brahmanic

From the remote past there has been a great controversy and a conflict of opinion among the scholars and the votaries of Brāhmanism regarding the relation between the Vedic and the Pāñcarātra teachings. The object of this paper is to analyse the possible causes for the unfavourable attitude of the orthodox brāhmaṇas towards the *Pāñcarātra*.

First, the Pāñcarātra was regarded by some of its followers as related to the Vedas, as root and trunk with its branches.[1] Śāṇḍilya, the promulgator of Pāñcarātra, being dissatisfied with the Vedas, not finding in them the quick and perfect way of attaining supreme excellence and final beatitude, had to take recourse to this *śāstra*.[2] The Vṛddha Hārīta[3] also informs that Śāṇḍilya composed a work for performing the worship of Kṛṣṇa by a non-Vedic procedure. Similarly, *Niśvāsatatvasaṁhitā*[4] describes how Vaśiṣṭha, unable to attain perfection by the performance of the Vedic rites, had to take lessons from Buddha in Tāntrism. It is corroborated in the Rūdrayāmala.

The Pāñcarātras attach more importance to their own sectarian scriptures than to the Vedas. The study of the Vedas is undertaken by them only for a mere acquaintance with the contents of these works. Aparārka[5] quotes a passage from a *saṃhitā* to show that the Pāñcarātras read the Vedas for the sake of mere knowledge.

Some of the Tantras, more specially the Śaiva and Śākta, declare the futility of the Vedas. The *Kulārṇavatantra*, for

1 Mahato vedavṛkṣasya mūlabhūto mahānayam
Skandabhūtā ṛgādyāste śākhābhūtāstathā mune.
Īśvara saṁhitā, 1. 24.

2 Brahma Sūtra, II-2-45.

3 II. 181-192.

4 H. P. Shastri, Cat. of palm leaf MSS. Darbāra library, Nepal, pp. 10, 137. Preface p. lxxvii.

5 Comm. on Yājñavalkya Smṛti.

example, says that for each age the Lord has given a suitable śāstra and in Kali age, Āgamaśāstra alone is suitable.[6] In *Kubjikātantra* also it is said that gods are pleased if they are worshipped according to the rules of the Tantras. The *Kākacuḍāmaṇi* tries to establish the superiority of Tantras to the Vedas by saying that the Vedas being very old in age cannot lead to perfection.[7] This we find in the *Varāhapurāṇa* and *Jamadagni-smṛti* as well, which are non-Tāntric works.[8] The *Kūlārṇavatantra* and the *Brahmajñānatantra* compare the Tantra to high born women and the Vedas to a public woman.[9] The Aparārka quotes from some unknown work the rule that one initiated in the Tantras should not follow the Vedic rules and rituals and *vice versa*.[10] So also *Vīraśaivānandacandrikā*[11] quotes some passages that purport to say that the followers of the Vedic and Tāntric path should not mix together, but should avoid each other. It also quotes a verse wherein it is maintained that those who fall away from the Vedic path should follow the Tāntric path.[12] The Pāñcarātra tantras are not as outspoken as the Śaiva and Śākta tantras. In the *Ahirbudhnyasaṃhitā* two methods of worship are referred to—one Vedic regarded as inferior which the other Pāñcarātra as superior. The Pāñcarātras had ever since emphasised this distinction.[13]

6 Kṛte śrutyuktācārastretāyām smṛtisambhava
Dvāpare tu purāṇoktam kalau āgama kevalam.

7 Vedānām ca vayo arthena na siddhistena jāyate.

8 Alābhe veda śāstrāṇām pāñcarātroditena hi.

9 Veda śāstra purāṇāni sāmānya gaṇikā iva
Yā punah śāmbhavi vidyā guptā kūla vadhuriva.
Kūlārṇava Tantra XI. 85.

10 Comm. On Yājñavalkya smṛti, 1. 7.
Dikṣitasya ca vedoktam śrāddhakarma vigarhiṭam
Iṭyevam vaidika śrāddhakriyā nādikṣitairapi.

11 Tantreṣu dikṣito martyo vaidikam na spraśetsadā.
Vaidikascāpi tantreṣu dikṣitam na sprasetsadā.

12 Veda mārga pracyutānam tantramārga praveśanam.

13 Trayīmārgeṣu niṣṇātāḥ phalavāde ramanti te
Devādineva manvānā na ca mām menire param.

The second reason to which the conflict of Pāñcarātra with the Brāhmanic authorities is due, is the predominance of the Tantric element in the Pāñcarātra. It is of non-Vedic origin. In its early stage it does not seem to have recognised the Vedic ideas and practices, *varṇāśramadharma* and the authority of Vedas, though in its later stage it could not ignore them.

The ideas, rites and practices of *Pāñcarātrasaṃhitās* amply testify to their non-brahmanical or rather anti-brāhmanical character. In the *Kūrmapurāṇa* the sects adhering to Tāntric rites and practices are condemned and Pāñcarātras included in them.[14]

The third reason for the condemnation of Pāñcarātra is the undue emphasis on image worship which is manifestly non-Vedic. In the *Brahmapurāṇa* it is said that the Sāttvatas were worshipping in the temples for their livelihood under the orders of kings.[15] Manu also avers the same.[16] The Sāttvatas were regarded as the fifth low caste people and since they used to make their living by worshipping images, they were dispised and regarded as low and disreputable. The *Āgama Prāmāṇya* states that the Sāttvatas (i.e. the Pāñcarātras) were looked down upon and nicknamed as 'devalaka' and that worshipping images was their hereditary business.[17] They were further regarded as unworthy to perform *yajña* and study scriptures.[18] Those who

14 I. 12. 256-8, I. 16. 115-7, I. 24. 31-3, I. 29. 25, II. 16. 15-6, II. 21. 32-3, and II. 37. 146-7.

15 Quoted in Āgama Prāmāṇya, p. 8.

16 Vaiśyāttu jāyate vrātyāta sudhanvācārya eva ca
Kāruṣasca vijanmā ca metrāḥ sāttvata eva ca
Pañcamo sāttvato nāma viṣṇoḥ āyatanam hi saḥ
Pujayedājñayā rājñām sa tu bhāgavata smṛta. X. 23.

17 (I) Devakoṣopajīvi yassadevalakocyate.
(II) Vṛtyartham pūjayet devam trini varṣāṇi yo dvijaḥ
Sa vai devalako nāma sarva karmasu garhitaḥ
Quoted in *Āgama Prāmāṇya*, p. 9.
(III) Vārāhamihira in Bṛhadsamhitā (60. 19) refer Bhāgavatas as worshipper of Viṣṇu temples.

18 Eṣām vamsa kramādeva devārcā vṛttito bhavet
Teṣāmadhyayana yajñe yājane nāsti yogyatā.

earn their livelihood by worshipping images are deprecated by Atri, Vyasa and other smṛti writers and prohibit even a look at their dead bodies.[19]

Yāmuna, the writer of *Āgama Prāmāṇya* urges that this popular view is not correct. He argues that though there are many Sāttvatas who make their living by worshipping images, not all of them take to professional priestly duties, and there are many who worship the images through pure devotion. Moreover, he quotes a verse from *Paramasaṃhitā* in support of his contention that those who make image to worship as their profession, do so only in the state of emergency.[20]

Fourthly, the religion of the Pāñcarātra is distinguished for its emphasis on divine love, exuberance of feeling and fervent emotion. In the Vedic school though devotion is given its due place, it was neither exaggerated nor made emotional. In some of the *Saṃhitās*, *bhakti* is even made an end in itself, *pañcama puruṣārtha*, higher than and superior to *mokṣa*, the latter being the side issue of the former. This was contrary to brāhmanic tradition and as such was strongly opposed.

Fifthly, the early *Saṃhitās* of Pāñcarātra show their indifferent and irreverent attitude to brāhmanic doctrines, practices and traditions. The Sāttvatas or Vṛṣṇis among whom it was prevalent, each aspersions against the Brāhmaṇas.[21]

Another cause of their denouncement was that the Pāñcarāttras admitted and initiated within their sect women and śūdras freely,

19 Ahvsayaka devalaka nakṣatra grām yājakaḥ
Ete brāhmaṇa cāndālā mahāpathika pañcamāḥ. Vyāsa.

20 Āpadyapi ca kaṣṭāyām bhito vā durgato'pi vā
Pūjayanneva vṛttyartham devadevam kadācana.

21 Arth Śāstra of Kautilya Ed. R. Shāmā Shāstri, p. 138.

Also the following:

Api ācaratasteṣāmabrāhmaṇyam pratīyate
Vṛttito devatā pūja dikṣā naivedya bhakṣaṇam
Garbhādhānādi dāhānta samskārāntara sevanam
Śrautakriyā ananuṣṭhānam dvijaissambandhavarjanam
Ityādibhiranācārairabrāhmaṇyam sunirṇayam.

Quoted in *Āgama Prāmāṇyam*, p. 8.

and they were allowed to worship Viṣṇu. This was manifestly contrary to the *varṇāśrama dharma* and Vedic authority and therefore was disliked in the brāhmanic circle. Manu, Yajña-valkya and Āśvalāyana smṛti, for example, prescribe that no one but an outcaste would therefore accept the *mantras* recommended by the Pāñcarātra. So much is the contempt for the Pāñcarātra that in the fourth chapter of the *Bṛhadnāradīyapurāṇa* it is said that even for conversation with the Pāñcarātras one would have to go to the Raurava hell. Similar opinion is also found in the *Kūrmapurāṇa.* The Sāttvatas were regarded as low caste people, outcaste, hybrid, originated from the Vaśyas, who had not the initiation with the holy thread.[22] Manu regards them as belonging to '*pañcamavarga*', even inferior to the Śūdras. The fact is that many of the Pāñcarātras were *śūdras,* and the political supremacy of the Śūdras, during Nanda and Maurya dynasties, further aggravated the situation.

Lastly, free admission of casteless foreigners into the Bhāgavata fold[23] and the encouragement to *sannyāsa* for the practice of *yoga,*[24] as contrasted with the conservative and orthodox view of the Brāhmaṇas, tend to show that the character of Bhāgavatism which was accepted by these foreigners must have been against *varṇāśrama dharma,* and therefore, a menace to it.[25] We may note that the author of smṛtis and purāṇas always warned people against disclosing the contents the holy books to such people.[26]

That the Pāñcarātra is non-Vedic, if not anti-Vedic, is evident from the *Mahābhārata* (*Nārāyaṇiya* sectioa XII. 335-351). Here we are told that the seven Citraśikhandin sages proclaimed it

22 Manu X. 23.

23 Besanagar Inscriptions also Bhāgavatapurāṇa II. 4. 18.

24 Artha Śāstra mentions spies disguised as ascetic with shaved head or braided hair and pretending to be the worshipper of God Samkarṣaṇa. (p. 403) cf. Mecrindle, Ancient India, p. 97.

25 Bhāgavatapurāṇa II. 4. 18, II. 7. 46, Visnu purāṇa V. 38. 28, Ibid IV. 24. 18.

26 Vārāhapurāṇa 103. 69-70.

which was on a par with the four Vedas[27] and was made consistent with them.[28] We do not know for certain whether there was any ancient Pāñcaratra work ascribed to these seven sages, but the very reference to making the scripture which was made conform to the four Vedas, is important in that it implies the originally non-Vedic, if not anti-Vedic, character of the ideas and practices of the Pāñcarātra. The *Mahābbhārata* itself admits that the Pāñcarātra system is different from the Vedic, for it says, "know, O saintly king, the Sāṁkhya, the Yoga, the Pāñcarātra, the Vedas and the Pāśupatas as knowledge holding different views".[29] In the *Mahābbhārata*[30] itself we get an indication that this new doctrine was recognised as opposed to the pure teachings of the Vedas.

These reasons perhaps were mainly responsible for the denunciation of and hatred against the Pāñcarātra school of Vaiṣṇavism.

27 XII. 335. 276-9.
28 XII. 335. 40.
29 XII. 349. 64.
30 XII. 269. 9.